actually
THINKING

vs.

just
BELIEVING

by
Doug Matheson

authorHOUSE®

AuthorHouse™
1663 Liberty Drive
Bloomington, IN 47403
www.authorhouse.com
Phone: 1-800-839-8640

First published by AuthorHouse 12/03/2010

ISBN: 978-1-4520-9510-3 (sc)
ISBN: 978-1-4520-9511-0 (e)

Library of Congress Control Number: 2010916017

Printed in the United States of America

Dedication

to Stephanie, Jonathan, Vanessa, and
all of the younger generation
who will inherit the nation, culture,
and world we leave them...
for better or for worse.

Acknowledgements

Time spent writing is preceded by time spent thinking and time spent reading. I thank my wife and children for their understanding of the moments I've been physically here but mentally elsewhere. And I thank my many outstanding, inquisitive, and demanding students who've kept me on my toes and made teaching even more worthwhile. You know who you are.

I would like to thank Gwyneth Cravens, Lorraine Davis, Carol Imani, Lynne LeBlanc, Lawrence Powers, Dennis Ross, and Tim Rowsell for reading drafts of this book and contributing their criticism, remarks, and suggestions.

There are several authors whose books I will recommend at the appropriate discussion points along the way. I thank them now for contributing to my learning and to the food for thought that I may be fortunate enough to pass on. They are: Richard Arum, Gwyneth Cravens, Richard Haass, Michael Pollan, Samantha Power, Scott Russell Sanders, Jeffrey Sachs, E. O. Wilson, and Fareed Zakaria.

Sincerely,
Doug Matheson

Table of Contents

Section I. Setting the Scene: Our Convictions, and Facing Our Problems

Section II: The Immediate & Long-term War Against Terrorism

Section III: America's Durable Internal Stability

Preface

"It was the best of times, it was the worst of times." These are familiar words from Dickens. My question for our consideration is: How are our times? Before taking the first step toward answering this, let me emphasize that we must look decades beyond this immediate political cycle. Realistically assessing the nature of one's "times" has historically required the benefit of hindsight. That no doubt, to some degree, is still true. However, in business, in sport, even in driving a car, real time assessment of your situation can mean the difference between success and failure, and even between surviving or not.

I submit that our times call for a serious effort to realize what our situation is without the delay of waiting for the perfect clarity of hindsight. Our times are a strange mix of privilege and peril. The 'privilege' part doesn't need much explanation; no matter if you are a newborn or a centenarian, life has never been easier or apparently more secure. I am convinced though, that the vast majority in our society haven't thoughtfully explored the 'peril' part, or begun to make committed decisions toward being part of the solution, not part of the problem.

Join me in doing what I call a "50 year experiment." Let's start by going back 50 years. In 1960 the Second World War was 15 years into our rearview mirrors. America led the world militarily, economically, technologically, scientifically; you could name almost any field. If you were a typical American family, with the exception of the background threat of the cold war, the future seemed bright well beyond the horizon. Your kids, grandkids, then great-grandkids and on would live in bigger and more luxurious houses, and they'd drive faster and cooler cars. It hadn't entered the public consciousness that there was actually a limit to fossil fuels (or that burning more and more of them would inevitably add up to some kind of slowly developing consequence); everyday folk had no idea that ecosystems, both terrestrial and marine, could be strained to the breaking point.

Now let's go forward 50 years. In 2060 how will things be? Keep in mind that next year the human population will hit 7 billion. Also keep in mind that when my mom was a 10 year old in 1930 and the human population hit 2 billion, no generation of people had ever lived through a doubling of the population. (The 1 billion mark had been reached in 1800.) Now my mom and her generation have lived through well over a tripling of the population. If we don't destroy ourselves first, we're projected to hit 8 billion by the mid '20s, and 9 billion well before 2060. What will that do to competition for basic survival resources?! Consider energy, water, arable land, food, jobs, and other vital factors. Further, what will it do to already strained ecosystems?

This isn't about despair and gloom, but it is about facing reality and beginning to do something about it. Imagine a doctor consulting with an obese 30 year old who has gained an average of 10 lbs a year since graduating from high school at 180 lbs. The doctor can tell this beer-, cigarette-, and football-lovin' 300 lb couch potato, "If you don't change your ways, you're dead by 40." Now, the doctor has made a prediction, but does it have to come true? What was the first word of his prediction? "If." So if the young man **does** change his ways, the outcome dramatically improves. Aha.

If we change our ways, this 50 year experiment also doesn't have to end in the very picture of ugliness.

We each have a natural tendency, an instinct, to be geared toward self-preservation. That is obviously not a bad thing. But when we unconsciously let that morph into the all-too-common "me, now" mentality of our current society, that spells trouble. We have been all about growing our 401Ks, accumulating toys and luxuries, being hip with style, wanting good Medicaid, Medicare, Social Security, and the world's strongest military, while, oh yeah, wanting low taxes. We have been all about 'growth,' with not a thought to 'sustainability.' We have wanted somebody else, in some place else or in some future time, to pay for our desired lifestyles today. Broadly, we have acted like ecosystems are infinitely stretchable or quickly repairable, or like future generations won't really miss what they never knew. We have pretended that a world of increasing inequity with major regions of poverty, ignorance, and despair will somehow remain a relatively stable world, and that the roots of terrorism will shrivel up as if by wishing it so. Far too many of our rich have believed that they somehow deserve their luxuries and don't owe society the same disproportionate generosity in return; far too many of our poor have believed that someone owes them a free ride; and far, far too many of all of us have put up with both of these mindsets.

While a bright future for mankind is possible, the grave for modern civilization as a whole is unfortunately also a distinct possibility. What keeps so many in our society from getting serious about the challenges of our time, and beginning to choose to be part of the solution? No doubt there are a variety of things, but certainly it includes: ignorance, by circumstance, but also by choice; simple preoccupation; our tendency to "believe what we're most comfortable believing;" our tendency to see the problems as "too big for me to make a difference;" and our belief, conscious or subconscious, that the solution to our natural or man-made problems is, in the end, supernatural. All of these lead to a failure to think, to analyze evidence, to reevaluate beliefs, to change our minds when it's called for, to choose and to act differently, to get way past the "me, now" mentality, and to recognize that we do owe a decent, stable, and enjoyable world (ecologically, sociologically, and economically) to future generations.

My friends, we are all in this boat together. We share the only habitable planet we know of, one ocean, and one atmosphere. We have to get beyond thinking of our individual freedoms in the good ole American way. We need to remember that the Founding Fathers wrote into the preamble to our Constitution that part of the very purpose to this new government was, "to promote the general welfare." Of course they weren't speaking of welfare checks, but they certainly were saying that we need to keep in mind what accomplishes the broader good, and not be solely preoccupied with "me, now."

In assessing our situation, we must learn to periodically if not regularly reevaluate our beliefs, and we must do this openly and honestly. This involves taking verifiable evidence more seriously, and it involves insisting with ourselves that our thought processes themselves be more objective. This must mean that we allow ourselves, and perhaps require ourselves, to change our minds when the evidence warrants it.

Young people are sometimes better at this than middle-aged adults. After a school-year-ending month of research and student presentations on "Challenges in the Next Half Century" my students have often asked, "What do we do?" We brainstorm briefly. It is interesting that on one hand we end up with a list of practical and concrete things from the tried and true three Rs (reduce, reuse, and recycle) to increasing use of alternative energy sources. On the other hand, inevitably some students point out something like, "But there are a whole lot of people who don't realize any of these challenges need to be faced." My next question for them is, "Why is that?" We end up discovering that before changes in behavior happen, changes in mindset must begin.

This book is about our mindsets and our future. We'll examine our biases, we'll deal with the real-world politics of terrorism and our foreign policy, and we'll delve into a variety of internal matters that will ultimately keep us a stable and sustainable nation and culture, or see us fragment and weaken into irrelevance, or even devolve into chaos.

Who am I to think I have something to add to the discussion of winning out over terrorism and maintaining a stable and sustainable society at home? Let me first say some of who I am not. I'm not an Ivy League graduate, I'm not a Washington insider, and I was not born to wealth or connections. I grew up a conservative Christian, went to graduate school at a regular state university, and I'm raising my family in small town America. Like scattered other middle-Americans though, I'm ending my silence and speaking up. Why I care about international issues and have the guts to speak out from small-town America has somewhat to do with my unusual background. I grew up in India as a missionary kid, went to high school in Singapore, and as an adult have lived and worked in Lebanon, Canada, France, and Rwanda. My experiences in Lebanon and Rwanda were particularly informative to my world view. Watching the fabric of civilization begin to unravel left me with a heightened concern for risks we face today and in the near future. Lessons I learned working in Lebanon and then travelling in the Middle East are a significant part of what I share in Chapters 3, 4, and 6; lessons learned while working in and then evacuating from Rwanda are most focused in Chapters 1 and 9. The breadth of my life experience, however, does not guarantee the correctness of what I assert any more than others being born to privilege guarantees what they assert; it is evidence and careful reasoning that should be used in evaluating anyone's assertions.

I have chosen to contrast simple truths with politics-as-usual in pretty direct words, thus you hold in your hands a compact book; it doesn't need to be long. Though I suspect that some may initially be offended, that is not my intent, and if they keep reading through the explanation and background to these truths, I think that many will get past feeling offended. Although on various particulars I have referenced specific sources, in general I have deliberately limited the interruptions of numerous citations; this is not a doctoral dissertation. My approach is rather to rely on common sense based on experience, a lifelong habit of asking questions and actually listening to answers, reading, and thinking rationally. My choice of informal voice, as if you and I were engaging in conversation, is deliberate; I hope it encourages you, my reader, to find venues in which to speak up. It is direct cut-to-the-chase truth backed by evidence that I hope will provide food for thought and a foundation for real dialogue.

My intended target audience is my fellow middle-Americans – people who read and think, who don't blindly vote any party line, but who have for too long been silent. We have let ourselves be polarized by extremists on either end of the political spectrum. The "squeaky wheels" at these extremes have dominated the discussion. It is time that we in the middle speak up and take responsibility for influencing policy. We don't want to be blindly ideological like some, we don't want to be intolerant, and we don't want to resort to violence. However, we most certainly do want to end our passivity. We can be radically activist for non-extremist positions. Even if you don't end up agreeing with me, end your silence. Participate in the public debate on how to strengthen our society and constructively interact with the dangerous world in which we find ourselves. Let's stop being silent followers of the supposed political elite — they can actually be pretty ignorant.

I have taken the risk of dealing fairly early in this book with our convictions, often based in religious belief, and the biases behind them. It is this contrast between *believing*, based on conscious choice or not, and analytically *thinking* that is the central theme of this book. We cannot begin to deal realistically with the myriad challenges of our time without first recognizing the influence of our philosophical starting points, and then learning to step beyond the shoes we happen to have grown up in. Note that at times this will inevitably mean hearing a point of view which we don't initially like. An important question to ask ourselves is: "When we don't like an idea, do we just stop in our tracks, reaffirm our prior belief, and think no further? Or, do we hear things out, weigh what evidence and logic is presented, and then allow ourselves to make a thoughtful decision?" That is for you to decide. I invite you to join the discussion.

Section I.
Setting the Scene: Our Convictions, and Facing Our Problems

Chapter 1.

Rwanda's Tragedy:
Lessons toward Re-evaluating *Belief*

That Thursday morning the quiet rest of our pre-dawn slumber was shattered by an instantaneous full-scale adrenalin rush. Machine-gun fire erupting twenty yards from your bedroom window is not your usual wakeup call. In one moment my unconscious thoughts had been mulling the events of the previous evening and few weeks; still, the night had been silent and my deep subconscious probably drew some reassurance from the occasional nursing sounds of my infant son who had awakened earlier and was now enjoying the comforts only a mom can provide. In that next moment, thought ceased; only reflex action was fully engaged.

It may be difficult to imagine just how quickly you can move when necessary. In an instant I had my wife and son away from our window and into the hallway; it only took one second more for me to get fifteen feet further down the hall and into our three and a half year old daughter's room. A second more and she, still wrapped in her sheets and fully draped in the mosquito net I had just torn from the ceiling, was in the relative safety of the hallway too.

Crouching in the pre-dawn darkness in the protection of a windowless hallway in a solid brick-and-mortar house, reflex action had nothing more to offer; thought could begin to gear up again. The machine-gun fire fairly quickly became sporadic, and then as dawn broke, it stopped in our immediate neighborhood. The renewed silence also helped my mental wheels start turning again.

Mixed in with our preoccupation with safety and survival, and with trivial necessities like diaper changes, the subsequent hours and days with nothing else to do provided a fair amount of time for thought. A few days and nights spent like that certainly allow for mental back and forth that is scattered to say the least. There we were, "muzoongooz" (foreigners) in the middle of a fight we certainly hadn't picked. We had arrived in Rwanda more than three years before as missionaries working for the Seventh-day Adventist church, though my work was not evangelism per se, but involved public health education and managing a network of five clinics in remote parts of the country.

We had gone to bed on Wednesday night knowing that Rwandan President Juvenal Habyarimana's plane had been shot out of the sky on approach to the airport that evening. I tried to reassure my wife of a few things: that in the months before that April day, the moves toward power-sharing multiparty democracy had been interrupted by a few other assassinations, but the general movement still had continued without chaos erupting; and that neither of the major sides in the conflict wanted to be blamed for killing, much less targeting, foreigners. Thus all we had to do was stay out of the crossfire. Spending much of our time on a mattress under a solid wood table we moved into one of our hallways seemed like a good start.

Taking stock of our situation I knew that we had sufficient water to last a few weeks, and we had enough basic food too. I had a battery-powered ham radio setup and so could keep in touch with key people, and to our surprise the phone continued to work throughout that day and one more night. Further information gathering, processing, and sharing became a high priority. The Rwandan Patriotic Front (RPF) rebels were indeed on the move from the north. In the outskirts of the capital Kigali, where we lived, the killing seemed very focused from both the formal and informal Hutu militia toward the Tutsi minority and Tutsi sympathizers. We had a fifteen-year-old Tutsi boy, Jackson, living with us and doing yard work in exchange for his tuition in a school for mechanics. He was clearly at risk. A hundred yards down the road from our gate was the entry to a compound with four other expat families and a dental clinic; none of those families had a ham radio.

In an extended lull with no fighting on Friday the Sri Lankan dentist Ranjan and I 'shouted,' in hushed tones if that's possible, back and forth from the nearest corners of our properties. His two sons had a set of walkie-talkies. Ranjan would run one of them halfway to my gate, and I'd run and meet him. From that point on I could pass on my ham radio communication to them via the little walkie-talkies.

On Thursday night we had received a call from one of my brothers back in the US. He seemed relieved to know we were staying reasonably comfortable and that I felt we were clearly not targets. We took some reassurance in the simple contact from the outside world that gave us concrete reminder that we were loved and cared for. Yes, we knew that our devoutly religious moms and others were praying for us, but I also knew that local people I knew and worked with were being butchered despite their and others' fervent prayers.

At first I thought cooler heads might prevail and we would get past the initial reflexive spasms of chaos and violence. By Friday night that was pretty much clearly not the trend. Via the ham radio we had a discussion with the US Ambassador David Rawson and the Adventist Development and Relief Agency (ADRA) director Carl Wilkens about a possible evacuation convoy. The idea was to head south to the neighboring country of Burundi on Saturday. I immediately shared this via walkie-talkie with the dental clinic compound families, including my personal hesitation to go. Having traveled a monthly route for over three years to the five scattered clinics I managed, I had seen frustrated villagers construct road blocks with fallen trees or by stacking rocks on 50 gallon drums for a variety of seemingly trivial reasons. Under the current circumstances I thought keeping our heads down for the moment beat trying to talk our way through roadblocks manned by agitated armed soldiers drunk on banana beer.

The seeming reassurance of not being a target can wear pretty thin quite quickly. Some time in a particularly quiet part of the middle of Friday night our older dog suddenly charged from our back porch, barking ferociously, toward our gate. While trying to gently and calmingly pat my wife's shoulder, I fully expected to hear machine-gun fire tearing through the thin metal of our gate to silence the dog whose barking was giving away someone's presence. For several long seconds the barking continued, and not a shot was fired. The next sound made my wife grab at me in the darkness, and it did silence the dog. A series of perhaps five or six quick sequential rocket launches ended in eerie silence. I lay there still patting my wife's shoulder, our two kids still sleeping peacefully.

My efforts to quietly reassure my wife gave no hint of what I was recalling. Over a decade before, while young and single, I had watched from a rooftop in east Beirut while opposing sides launched rocket attacks on each other. I had seen how one side would use the obvious launch site of their enemy's rockets as their next target for return rockets. At this moment in Rwanda, despite having strong walls around our hallway fortress, lying there with only a solid wood table and a sheet-metal roof over our heads, I did not like the thought of incoming returning rockets. Needless to say, I kept this thought to myself.

On Saturday we awaited word of what would happen to the small evacuation convoy that had headed south to Burundi. I fretted over what options I had with our young sponsored student, Jackson. I already knew that if we evacuated we'd have to pass through multiple road blocks. The genocide had begun, the official and unofficial militias were looking for Tutsis. Yet leaving him alone at the ripe old age of fifteen seemed unimaginable. I felt responsible for him, but there were no good options.

With this running through my head, I heard my immediate neighbor to the north calling out quietly to me over the brick wall that separated our yards. We had been friendly neighbors, but I only knew him superficially. He was a diplomat from Burundi, a member of the Tutsi minority, and had his own young family. I went up close to the wall where we could talk without attracting attention, and where I could look him in the eye. The jagged broken glass embedded in concrete that topped the wall was at about chin level on both of us. He said he knew he was asking a lot, but because things were deteriorating further, could he and his family join us in our house.

My instinct was of course yes, but I told him I would want to talk with my wife. I walked slowly back inside.

On one hand I felt like this should be an easy decision, but running through my mind was an experience from only a few months earlier. Because of some apparently local unrest, a decision had been made to evacuate the boarding students off the campus of the Adventist university in the northwest and down to Kigali. It was felt that having some expats involved in the evacuation would help the process run smoothly and safely. Carl Wilkens, the ADRA director, and I were asked if we would help.

In the process of that evacuation, Carl and I were put at substantial risk to protect one particular student. We took the risks, and the student survived. It was later that I found out that the student's own words and actions in the previous weeks had been inviting trouble.

To the best of my knowledge my neighbor hadn't been inviting trouble. Still, I was keenly aware that my knowledge of my neighbor was very limited, and decisions based on limited information are never easy. My wife thought that a family with young children needed protection, so we agreed to take them in.

Before going back to talk with my neighbor I checked in on the ham radio and received the good news that the convoy had made it safely to Burundi. Further, Ambassador Rawson was in the process of planning another one to leave Sunday. I got on the walkie-talkie and relayed the news, and my recommendation to go this time. I then rejoined my neighbor at the wall.

He was visibly relieved to hear that they were welcome to join us in our house. His relief went even deeper when I told him the first evacuation convoy had made it, and that we were forming a second one to leave the next morning. He wanted to get back to his home country. We decided to wait till shortly after dark to have his family come over.

That evening I checked in on the radio several times.

The list of those joining the second convoy grew. It required a bit less than a full tank of fuel to make it to Burundi, but many families didn't have full tanks, and obviously there were no functioning gas stations. I had a full tank and two jerry cans full to share. Still, we quickly realized that the only available and substantial supply of gas and diesel was in two large tanks on the US embassy grounds near downtown.

Those tanks had backup manual pumps, so the absence of electricity wasn't a problem. The trick would be trying to arrange a temporary ceasefire for a convoy of expats to get to downtown, have time to fuel up, and then get out of town. The ambassador would work on it.

That evening Carl Wilkens indicated that while his wife, kids, and his visiting parents would evacuate, he would not. As ADRA director he felt his job called him to be active in just such emergencies. We lived only about a mile from Carl's house, and none of that distance required traveling on a main road. I asked him, assuming we could get Jackson to him, if Jackson could stay with him. He readily agreed.

The ambassador had stated that the jet that would fly us out of Burundi would need to have a priority on people, not baggage, so limit what you pack! As my wife gathered irreplaceables like home videos, one change of clothes for us, some extras for our kids, plus diapers for our youngest, I talked quietly with Jackson. We had no way of knowing whether his family was dead or alive. We hoped, but I could see in his eyes that he feared the worst. I explained that we were going to try to leave the country, and I wanted to help leave him in the safest situation I could. He seemed to understand that if we tried to take him with us, we almost certainly wouldn't make it through the check points with him; he would be taken and killed. He understandably didn't want to run that risk.

I brought up Carl Wilkens' offer, but Jackson seemed reluctant. I pointed out that I could leave him with plenty of basic food and he had plenty of water in the tank, and that he could stay in his small but solid guest house in our yard. Our two dogs might help provide some security. That seemed his preferred choice.

We bedded our neighbors down in our other hallway, and tried to get some rest. The night was quiet and uneventful, but except for the kids, I don't think we actually slept at all. My mind churned and churned.

At times I reflected on the notions of the God I had grown up with. My dad was an educator and my mom a nurse. When I was seven they had accepted what they felt was a call from God and had taken my four siblings and me to India where they worked for the Seventh-day Adventist church. I had been educated through my Bachelors degree in these private Christian schools. In preparing for and then beginning my own career as a science teacher, I had tried to resolve the contradictions between what my church in particular and Christianity in general held to be true, and what the evidence seemed to indicate. I wanted there to be a loving, wise, insightful, fair, just, and good God. I wanted to believe that evil was best explained by the devil and his agents operating within the system of freedom of choice that I hoped this good and non-manipulative God functioned in.

My graduate school experience in a secular university had prepared me for my Rwandan work in the field of public health, and it had also continued to broaden the array of questions I entertained about life, human nature, and the broader universe. I lay there that night and remembered the few times a clinic head nurse had shared with me that he had had patients with no diagnosable disease, but who spiraled downward because of a 'curse.' Some of these patients even died. I had asked this Western-medicine-trained nurse (who really functioned as a doctor in terms of diagnosing and treating) if he was aware of the power of belief, of the influence of the mind on the body. He had indicated that he was aware of it. I had then asked if he thought the same curse would work on me. He wasn't sure.

I had wanted him to be able to help 'sick' patients break the spell of belief. For some, prayer seemed to work, but not for all. Still, I wondered if that was much more than one form of black magic used to block another form. I knew that cavemen, and even more recent people, had ascribed mystical, supernatural, and spiritual explanations to eclipses, comets, lightning, the 'miracle' of birth, the tragedy of death, and any unexplained phenomena from a child's diarrhea to a drought or flood. I had asked that nurse to have one of the reputedly skilled curse-givers apply one on me. At first it was incredulity, then simply "No." I persisted. Finally, with what looked like a slightly amused smile, he agreed. I asked him if he thought the curse would or wouldn't work. He said he kind of doubted it. I asked why not. He said he thought it was because I didn't believe it would. I lay there that night and remembered wondering if that was progress. I also remembered asking him to go ahead and have the curse placed on me, just so we could complete our little test.

Over time I had opportunity to see that we humans had plenty of capacity for ugly nasty evil, and for noble good. And it seemed that we each had some measure of each, even if sometimes in far from equal proportions. Sometimes circumstances brought one side or the other to the fore, but it seemed to me that more often we tended to choose to cultivate one or the other tendency.

I also saw that one's basic beliefs about God, whether measured in broad type of religion joined (if *any* religion was joined) or simply which verses were preferred and emphasized, depended on one's life circumstances, educational level, and even personality type.

I wondered how co-workers, fellow church members, neighbors, in-laws, friends, or even strangers could turn on each other with such deadly intent.

I saw that natural instincts and the realities of competition for basic survival resources were facts that could be constructively managed and channeled – or manipulated and twisted.

I had many more questions than answers, but I had become 'okay' with functioning while letting several pots simmer unfinished on the back burners of my mental stove.

Sunday morning came and I got back on the radio for final, specific, convoy plans. We tried to convince Carl to evacuate too. No success. I shut the radio off for the last time. Then we hugged a scared young man – or do I call him a mere boy? – goodbye. I tried to will him confidence and courage, and he tried to put on a brave face, but trembling lips are lousy liars. (We tried to learn his fate when the chaos had ended over three months later, but nobody seemed to know. We didn't learn anything for almost fifteen years. He had survived; a story in itself!)

The convoy formed at the ambassador's residence within a half mile of our place. The ambassador's wife was to be part of the convoy. Our neighbor had retrieved his car from his yard, and his family was ready to go. Of course there were families I had never met too. The Wilkens family said their goodbyes. We were given one piece of roadblock advice: if you might visually be mistaken for a Belgian, don't let on that you speak or even understand French; just reply in English. We headed for the embassy fuel tanks downtown.

The arranged ceasefire seemed to hold. We snaked our way through roadblocks without delay or question. Moving at slow speeds, we felt no need to use child safety seats. My wife was holding our baby, and I was okay with our daughter moving freely and even standing up. Then I saw the first pile of dead bodies by the roadside. I instantly told her "Keep your head down." She was at the right age to have replied "Why?" before complying, but even at such a young age she knew too well that these weren't normal days. She squatted down without hesitation and then looked up at me and asked "Why daddy?" And when I honestly replied that there were things I didn't want her to see, she stayed right down there.

Fueling up one vehicle at a time by manual pump seemed to take forever, but we were finally ready to head for Burundi. On the down-slope, almost out of town, our convoy came to our first roadblock where they actually made us stop. The militia was letting one vehicle through at a time. While waiting in line, roving groups of young men, mostly armed with machetes, would go from car to car demanding "Amafaranga!" (money). We smiled and pretended to not understand, and my wife kept handing out generous handfuls of raisins and almonds we had taken from our now thawing freezer. The young men often smiled back with a polite "Meracozay" (thank you). Finally the whole convoy cleared the roadblock.

Not far out of town, just before crossing over the Nyabarongo River, I had to tell my daughter to keep her head down again. She did, and my wife and I watched a dump truck loaded to the hilt with dead bodies merge for only a short bit with our convoy. We quickly passed it, and

I watched in my rearview mirror as it began to dump the bodies in the river.

Perhaps about four hours later we crossed the border into Burundi. We breathed our first sigh of relief in five days. My internal tension let up, a bit.

Not too far across the border, with tropical darkness quickly falling, our neighbor, ahead of us in the convoy, pulled off to the roadside and waved goodbye as we passed. The Adventist church had rented a large vacant house in the capital city Bujumbura for several families to share that night. We tried to sleep, but we knew that the ethnic mix in Burundi was essentially identical to that of Rwanda, and that the tensions had to be high in Bujumbura.

On Monday morning we were told to go to the airport where a US Air Force jet was going to fly a bunch of expats to Nairobi, Kenya. Once at the airport we were told to, what else, wait. A bunch of young Marines recognized stress and degrees of fatigue in the faces of the adults. They figured they could help us relax by entertaining the kids. Knowing we had to be hungry too, they brought us an assortment of MREs with their personal recommendations of, "this is almost like mom's home cookin'," or "now try this if you want to, but frankly it's a lot like dog s***."

On boarding the jet we were seated in one of the long rows that ran the length of each side, and handed ear plugs. With almost no further delay we were off the ground and climbing steeply. After two or three minutes of steady altitude gain I squeezed my wife's knee; "We're out" I said right into her ear, and then involuntarily exhaled. She nodded, her eyes watery. There was no window to look out, but I could picture so well the land below to our left. I knew a lot of people who weren't out and really had nowhere to go.

In Nairobi we went into a prolonged 'wait' mode. During the week we spent in a hotel there we watched a lot of TV coverage about what was going on back in what had been our adopted home country. It seemed that fear was being used to get people to believe that their security and survival was being threatened, to believe that Tutsis were subhuman, to believe that it was either kill them now or later they will kill you. It seemed that those promoting these beliefs had one thing in mind – increasing and keeping power.

At the end of that week church administrators decided that the storm in Rwanda wasn't blowing over, so it was time to repatriate everyone. Since my wife's family was near Montreal, Canada, we asked for it as our temporary destination.

After a few days there, the church authorities informed us that the evacuated employees were being asked to participate in a debriefing/group therapy session in Virginia.

It was good to see those colleagues again, even if after only a relatively short separation. Some had worked in different parts of Rwanda, had gotten out by different means, and had experienced very different levels of closeness to horror.

Among the things that stick in my memory from those meetings were some rather tough experiences that a few had gone through. One couple from the university campus recounted watching with a Tutsi from inside their house as a mob of machete-wielding teenagers chased two Tutsi young ladies toward their house. They knew that if they opened the door to rescue those two, they and the third Tutsi inside their house would probably be butchered. In that moment they decided to keep the one already hidden in their house safe; they didn't open the door, and they had to listen to the final screams of two young women mixed with sounds of machetes in flesh until silence fell and the mob left.

Another thing that sticks in my mind is how many times someone in our group of evacuees thanked God for answering prayer and seeing them safely out. I remember trying gently to remind us that many other prayers had gone and were continuing to go unanswered. I tried to suggest that there was nothing wrong with simply being grateful to have survived, but that crediting God for it was in a peculiar way egotistical. Were we somehow more *special* than Rwandans in God's eyes?

I kept most of my questions and doubts to myself; they were unwelcome and perhaps not even constructive in the context of people trying to get back on their emotional feet. It was becoming increasingly clear that it is human nature to believe what each of us happen to want (or need) to believe.

As I looked back on my few years of health and development work and the chaos that ended our time in Africa, as I spent the next few days enjoying a reunion with my sister and her family in Richmond, and as I let TV and reading update me on current American culture and politics, I saw in steps of progressive clarity that *thinking* seemed to constantly be subservient to *believing*.

This brings me to the first simple truth I will share in this book.

Simple Truth # 1. The intensity of any belief, or its majority status, clearly says nothing about it being an evidence-supported or constructive idea.

I began to realize that the scale of challenges we humans face calls for recognizing tough realities without sanitizing them with the whitewash of cherished belief. I realized that first of all I had to make a greater personal commitment to being intellectually honest, to facing truths that at the gut level I might not want to.

As we put months between us and the Rwandan

genocide, I first wanted to simply find a safe and good environment in which to raise my family. But as the years ticked by and as I saw the rise of terrorism and our assorted responses to it, I realized anew the gulf between belief and hard, honest thinking. This gulf shows its face in so many facets of life.

Of course no two people have identical journeys from a starting point of loyally holding their beliefs toward the cultivated habit of thinking critically, and I realize that my path is different than usual (if there is such a thing). I have deep respect for several good acquaintances who, through nothing more than reading and thinking, have learned to limit the power of their inherited beliefs, and to think objectively. The unfortunate fact is that too many, well this side of remote and uneducated third world villages, hardly get started on their way. In the hope of ultimately helping us better address some of today's challenges, allow me to share some more from my experience on this journey. My growth and progress didn't start on any identifiable day, and it certainly hasn't ended. Still, Rwanda's tragedy was one of the bigger catalysts for my re-evaluation of *belief*.

Chapter 2.

Is Being "A Man of Conviction" Enough?:
Our Loyalties, What Drives Them, and
Alternatives to the Tendency to Fight

The two retired-looking gentlemen were talking in the canned goods section of a local grocery store as I searched for a few more items. I couldn't help but hear the scorn they heaped onto the very idea that there is any such thing as global warming. "Christ," said the one wearing suspenders, "they just need to step outside today for a reality check." For sure, it was a cold day in April of 2006; a few snow flurries had blown about that morning. But even more surely, those two gentlemen knew what they were going to believe, period.

This was just one among many instances which bring home the reality that most of us arrive, fairly shortly into adult life if not earlier, with a particular view of life. The intensity with which many hold the various views they inherited or chose is in itself an interesting phenomenon. I remember an otherwise rational, educated, local leading citizen being reduced to an obscenity-uttering, red-faced name-caller when discussing a recent presidential candidate. Why the intensity? Why the unwavering loyalty to one set of ideas, and absolute commitment to opposing an alternative set? Why indeed?

In the days of cavemen, being loyal to the clan's notions and opposing other ideas and ways was the norm. This is completely understandable. Education, leading to rational, analytical, and independent thinking, didn't exist. It is not only understandable, it was also constructive in that loyalty to *any* set of ideas contributed to the very survival of the clan because it unified the members. Thus the distant origins of 'blind loyalty' aren't hard to understand; natural selection has long favored traits, physical or behavioral, which contribute some survival advantage. But the persistence of blind loyalty in a generally educated and somewhat diverse culture is considerably harder to understand.

Some might quickly say that the same unifying survival value applies to today's larger national or cultural 'clans.' I would point out though that the potential hazards to clan warfare today are simply far too great to passively accept as "how we are wired." If you question this, consider that the world population is expected to hit seven billion next year and keep climbing, thus driving up competition for resources of every kind. At the core of cultural clan loyalty is the risk that the war on terror could broaden, deepen, and intensify into modern crusades. This is infinitely worse when we bear in mind that despite our efforts, weapons of mass destruction are in relative abundance. To all of this add the increasingly urgent need to deal with ecological issues from a global perspective. Indeed, the clan togetherness mentality has quit being a survival tool, and has crossed over to being a destructive risk. So why does it persist? After a few more points we'll get there.

We, at least in developed countries, are an incredibly privileged generation. In so many ways our lives are 'easy' far beyond our moment-to-moment recognition. We owe a debt of gratitude not only to the tough generation who worked their way through the depression and then saved the world from Nazism, but also to every clever scientist or persistent tinkerer who directly or indirectly contributed to basics like electricity and clean drinking water, or to high tech magic like sophisticated medical imaging and satellite communications. Much further back, we can be grateful some cavemen tamed fire and developed stone tools to the point of ensuring our survival. We owe them all.

What we owe to people in the past pales though in comparison to something else we owe. **We owe, in the most serious and intense meaning the word can carry, a decent, stable, and enjoyable world to generations yet to come. On this we must not fail!**

No generation before us has had nearly such a great degree of both access to vast amounts of raw information and the tools to analyze it all. There really is no excuse for continuing to hang on to various ancient precepts if we are going to let those ideas lead to shortsighted decision-making. Nor has any generation before us had such powerful potential to perhaps irreparably screw things up. In times of such a strange mix of privilege and peril, what we owe to our descendants ought to be the drive and focus of our lives. It should shake us out of the complacency of living simply for the moment and purely for ourselves. The sizes of our 401Ks aren't going to matter much if we allow cultural conflict to mushroom or ecological degradation to spiral downward.

So, we must look at blind loyalty's persistence in our midst today more critically than as just "how we are wired." Our brain power, whether seen as the gift of an all-mighty God or the end result of millennia of natural selection, *allows* us to analyze our tendencies, and what we owe to our descendants *obligates* us to analyze and then to overcome destructive tendencies.

It seems almost as though there is some unseen diversion

which side-tracks us from developing the *ability* and then the *tendency* to openly consider, and then rationally analyze new evidence, information, and ideas. This is, after all, where "education," not "indoctrination," should lead us. How do we continually end up in the ditch of blind loyalty when we need to stay on the pavement of openness to new or different ideas and rational analysis of verifiable evidence? And ultimately, how do we do better than believing what we *want* to believe?

I am on the verge of suggesting something that I have very mixed feelings about putting into words. My angst isn't about thinking the thought, it is about expressing the thought and thereby taking candy away from a toddler. If you're going to end up with a very upset baby, and one who can not only fuss but also make considerable trouble, you better have a very good reason for disturbing the peace. Until very recent years, I opted for not disturbing sleeping babies. I know others have made the suggestion I'm about to, but now I'm joining them. Why? Because the risks of passive silence in today's world are too great. And the more directions from which we get the uncomfortable and unwanted truths, the more likely that those truths will eventually sink in, take root, and make a difference.

Despite our educated status, where do we get our willingness to be side-tracked by this unnoticed diversion? With innately curious minds, how do we get so practiced at ignoring what we don't happen to *want* to believe?

Let me first answer this with the following illustration. Nutritional supplements, unlike medications, don't have to be rigorously tested in double blind studies. Manufacturers advertise based on anecdotal evidence which sounds good, and consumers give it a try, hoping for positive results. 'Hope' and 'belief' are powerful forces. Enough customers experience what they're looking for to keep them coming back for more. The fact that it may be the placebo effect is not a real problem.

Or is there a problem? Imagine that a particular herbal supplement reputedly helps lower blood pressure. What if an individual's belief in this supplement's reported effect keeps him from making the best decisions about his life choices? If he keeps smoking, or keeps eating so many saturated trans-fats, or continues to carry his excess weight, or continues his comfortable sedentary habits, does that constitute a problem? Further, if this unproven (and sometimes unprovable) supplement causes people to spend considerable resources, is the problem worsened? I trust the answers are obvious.

So, where do we get our training and practice at diverting ourselves from real evidence and ignoring what we don't happen to want to believe? What is this anecdotally supported but undemonstrable supplement that is possibly a placebo which keeps many from making the tough and responsible choices in life? It is religion. This is almost certainly **the least welcome but most needed statement I make.** If you feel like you just can't stand this idea, take a moment to remember the question you briefly considered near the end of the preface. "When we don't like an idea, do we just stop in our tracks, reaffirm our prior belief, and think no further? Or, do we hear things out, weigh what evidence and logic is presented, and then allow ourselves to make a thoughtful decision?"

The recognition that religion helps cultivate in us the tendency to *simply believe* is troubling, and it may still not get real traction, but the more people that realize it and find ways to share this insight, the more we can avoid some major unnecessary pitfalls that could trip up humanity. It may take more than another century, even in the age of computers and an incredibly shortened doubling time for information, but eventually people may look back and wonder why it took so long to get it. In the mean time, even an idea rejected with vehemence by some may still play a part in generating discussion – discussion which eventually can yield a change in thinking and critical decision-making. The worrisome aspect of this is that we may or may not have a full century of semi-peaceful and constructive existence and progress; more on this shortly.

Yes, we learn from a very young age that our various religious creeds are something we simply accept and believe. Any little "tests" of God are not only unverifiable, but are completely subjective. If what we believe makes us feel better (have less guilt through forgiveness, have meaning, hope, and such) that's good enough. We learn, consciously or subconsciously, that evidence doesn't really matter, that whatever we are told or what we want to believe is just fine and shouldn't be challenged. Faith or belief, those abstract notions by which we are willing to be guided, can even have the result of helping us shrug off individual responsibility for the practical results of our choices. We grow very comfortable in the ditch of blind loyalty, and very resistant to getting back on the pavement to learning and progress if it means accepting evidence we don't happen to like. Religious faith gets us started down the path of blind loyalty.

Return with me for a moment to the herbal supplement some take to help lower their blood pressure. Notice that the problem is not with the consumer's 'belief' that it helps; the problem is with irresponsible and shortsighted choices which are made with the 'belief' in the supplement as the backdrop. Our religious beliefs can form a backdrop to collective decisions we make – decisions which are critical considering some of the risks we face.

Among the various risks which we humans face, but about which we could actually do the most, several stand out to me. The first is that the war on terror will degenerate into a cultural war in which all of humanity would be the loser. Before you dismiss this, consider that with the attitudes of many, we may well be only a single successful large-scale terrorist attack (like the April 2007 JFK gas pipelines threat or the May 2010 attempted Times Square bombing could have been) away from a knee-jerk reaction that would plunge us into a poorly focused war on everybody who just subscribes to the 'wrong' set of beliefs or may simply not look like 'us.' A repeat of the Crusades is a real risk if we don't analyze our beliefs and tendencies ahead of time. The second is the risk that we degrade our environment so badly that our planet no longer has balanced, sustainable ecosystems. The third is the risk that we continue our long-standing and deeply ingrained habit of deficit spending, thus continuously adding to our national debt – a debt that, short of revolution and chaos, will actually have to be paid back. I have had the misfortune (or, from a learning perspective, the privilege) of watching, twice in my life, as the society around me came unraveled and degrees of chaos reigned. We don't have to keep ignoring things until these risks are realities. In terms of timing, the risk that the war on terror could become a poorly focused cultural war is completely uncertain, but could be sudden. The ecological and economic risks are much more like the proverbial frog in the slowly heating water – with the end result no less ugly. The central point here is that these risks are made worse by a certain type of faith-based thinking.

I am keenly aware that some will perceive this as another attack on religion in general and Christianity in particular, and that this "attack" couldn't be further from politically correct, or popular. I feel compelled to emphasize that I recognize religion as something near and dear to the heart of many; and in normal times I wouldn't be making any remotely critical comments on faith at all. But these are not normal times.

Remember our 50 year experiment in the preface. Imagine what people in 1960 were facing, what they knew, and what they looked forward to. WWII was recent past; Europe was re-stabilizing; a limit to supplies of energy from oil hadn't entered our consciousness; American science, industry, education, military power, culture, and our economy led the world; American families were busy making babies and thus the baby boom; developing countries were just beginning to develop, and their populations were beginning to really boom; the resources of forests, oceans, and prairies seemed limitless and beyond disruption; and our influence seemed without peer. Other than the Cold War's mutually assured destruction backdrop, the everyday-man confidently raised his family planning on his kids living easier lives, having ever-better medical care, and with those kids working or studying hard they would in turn create a bright future for themselves and eventually for his grandchildren. The perceivable future seemed bright.

Now we look forward 50 years from our point in history. Many today seem to assume that there is a future of constant improvement in quality of life for their kids too. But is this indefinitely realistic? As our global population moves past seven toward nine billion, what is that going to do to the demand for energy, for jobs, for arable land, for food, and for water? What will it do to pollution production and management? What will it do to the ever-increasing level of disconnect young people have from food production and other meaningful labor connections to real life? What will it do to the tendency toward conflict and war? What will it do to the gulf between the rich and the poor, especially with those terms viewed globally, not just nationally? What will it do to the balance, stability, and bio-diversity of ecosystems everywhere, both terrestrial and marine? Undeniably, we are past normal times.

Don't get the impression that I'm a hopeless pessimist. I think of myself as an action-oriented optimist. All of those problems become insurmountable only if we ignore them, squabble over them, or think and act like they're actually irrelevant because something supernatural will rescue us anyway. If, on the other hand, we take our responsibility and opportunity seriously, we can overcome each of those problems and actually leave our descendants a bright future, but it is going to take acting rationally, collectively, less self-ishly, and urgently. (On the theme of optimism, allow me to recommend Scott Russell Sanders' *Hunting for Hope*. It is practical, yet written so beautifully that it lifts your inner self too.)

No, I am **not** trying to start a campaign to stamp out religion. In fact, nothing would ensure its survival more certainly than such an attempt. Surely we can all be com-fortable in acknowledging that faith and belonging to some faith-based group or something like it does serve to meet some undeniable felt needs. In a society which appears almost infinitely large from any local perspective, we need sub-groups in which we feel we belong. Boy or Girl Scouts, volunteer groups from the United Way to the rural fire dis-trict, book clubs, the golf and country club, the "band" that may never play a gig beyond the garage, teams of all kinds, unfortunately gangs, and yes churches; in a way they all meet this need. Further, the painfully evident fact that "life isn't fair" is handled by many with the hope of a compensat-ing afterlife. And when the general unfairness of life turns downright devastating as in a tragic and premature death, the hope of an afterlife becomes almost essential to our san-ity. Even when we have just badly screwed up our own lives, the thought of a re-run is pretty appealing. This is all very real and in some ways can be seen as constructive.

We could have a whole side-discussion on the adaptability of religion too. Witness some branches of modern Christianity's convenient theme that God wants us to be rich, to drive fancy lifted 4-wheelers emblazoned with "Jesus Saves." Oh – never mind the irony of wearing a WWJD bracelet while showing off and guzzling gas. But let's leave religion's adaptability as a whole other discussion for another day.

What I *am* advocating is that people of faith recognize that just as their faith cannot be disproved, it also can't be proved. Considering that, let's all begin making practical decisions (ecological, political, and fiscal, both personal and collective) about life based on sound analysis of actual facts. We can't afford to continue to let preferred beliefs cause poor decisions.

What kind of preferred beliefs get in the way of sound decisions?

Simple Truth # 2. At the core, strong religious belief predisposes us to the unconscious thought that "There is a supernatural solution to our problems. We really don't have to worry over things because God will work out His will after all anyway."

Because I can't prove there isn't a supernatural solution to our problems, I am willing to say "Maybe there is." In return I hope someday we will reach the point when most believers will also admit "Maybe there isn't," and then follow a realistic assessment of the limitations of their hopes, and make decisions that are aimed at leaving the best possible real world to future generations.

I remind you that our times are indeed a strange mix of privilege and peril. We can't simply enjoy our easy lives and assume that the future is in God's hands. That would be like buying a lottery ticket and then, turning the 'possibility' that you *might* win into 'faith' that you *will* win, living it up even before the numbers are drawn. Who would be so foolish and shortsighted? Failing to take responsible action based on the belief that there will be a supernatural solution to our problems is equally shortsighted and foolish, and is the definition of presumption. No, we can't let the hoped-for soon-return of Jesus Christ keep us from making the tough and responsible choices today.

Fortunately it is a minority who are so fundamentalist and absolute about their faith that they consciously take the position that "God will save us, so who cares about the condition of the world?" Many good Christians take their stewardship of the planet and of their fellowman fairly seriously. In these cases the thought that "God will save us, so practical, tough, and inconvenient solutions aren't truly urgent" is much more subconscious, but no less real. A part of the basic problem in this case is that the almost subconscious decisions we make result in a misplacement of resources.

Imagine for a moment all the resources (manpower, material, and money) spent on various religious endeavors. Now imagine if everyone who chooses to continue investing those resources in religious ways also chose to invest equally and energetically in promoting real solutions from the tried and true 'reduce-reuse-recycle' concept to new and exploratory energy alternatives. It would be different.

The funny thing about this discussion is that for some, the perceived threat to their faith will make them react by hanging on to it with even greater irrational intensity. That's a risk we must take. I have been forced to the conclusion that it is a responsible citizen's duty to be willing to make comfortable people uncomfortable, to gently confront them with logic and evidence.

The irony is that the people who most need to be shifted out of absolute blind loyalty to their particular set of beliefs are the very people who are least likely to be reading this. Strangely, it comes back to an initially smallish group of inquiring minds who scan far and wide in the search for real ways of fulfilling what we owe to future generations. But then, big shifts have historically happened from small starts. So how do we get started? What do we do?

We can't wait for leaders of vision to discuss hard truths which a majority doesn't want to hear. That would be truly exceptional for a politician, perhaps simply because they understand that too much truth would result in them being shown the door. We can't sit around and wait for a clear majority, one which realizes the truth in the idea that religion has often caused shortsighted decisions, to develop. Rather, we must simply begin to get more of our fellow citizens to join us in making practical decisions with more than "me, now" or "God will fix it" at the core. Sound impossible?

I hope not. Engaging enough of the general population to form an insightful, committed, and effective block will be challenging. Filled with independent thinkers as this group would be, it would never be as unified as the committed religious right; blind loyalty to any cause or group is exactly what we are *not* trying to develop. We can and must though, come to outnumber or out-influence blind believers.

At this point in time it is easy to imagine a good, hard-working traditional farming family or busy suburban couple saying something like, "Who are you kidding? I love my God and country, and don't really pay much attention to what's going on in Timbuktu. I have no real reason to think that things aren't going to go on pretty much as they have been for generations, and my grandchildren have every likelihood of a good and normal, even great life." In honestly evaluating how realistic this lack of worry and commitment to action is, let's remind ourselves of several things.

Broadly, whether we like it or not, we do live in a global village. We might like imagining that America is self-sustainable and our lifestyles could continue in isolation, but if you just consider where we get the fuel to drive our tractors and heat our homes, you realize we are interdependent with others. The list of things we could add to energy interconnectedness is very long if you pause to reflect. We share one atmosphere, one ocean, and even if some families stay "local" to the point of a hermitage, "we" as a people travel and do business, and we cross cultural paths in constructive or destructive ways.

Unless you are willing to become a tree-hugger who lives like a caveman of old, isolationism isn't an option today. We must face up to constructive engagement with the rest of humanity scattered all across our fair planet. Wishful thinking no longer cuts it. It's not enough to have confidence that "our God" is the right one; our worst enemies think that way too. It's not enough to have the subtle, calming, and comfortable thought that "If it happened, it must be within God's will; ultimately He's got things under control." Man-made calamities have happened before, and that general risk isn't decreasing with time.

So, if it's not impossible to begin to get enough of our fellow-citizens nudged out of faith-based passiveness and inaction, how do we start?

We start by (1), completely embracing the notion that we really do owe to future generations a decent, stable, and enjoyable world. (2) Accepting the necessity of making comfortable people uncomfortable. (3)

Learning to engage and if necessary gently confront individuals in our natural circle of acquaintances; we use evidence and logic. (4) Sharing clear, persuasive information (allow me here to suggest the great little book *The Creation* by E.O. Wilson; it is written directly to conservative Christian leaders, and is about our collective responsibilities on planet earth). And (5), acknowledging and helping spread the notion that if we are not part of the solution, then we are part of the problem.

Allow me to share a few experiences from my journey of engaging people within my sphere of influence; hopefully these may also serve to make a few broader points. A few years ago, in the process of helping my students review for a state science test, we came across a practice question on how the earth formed. Before we could begin to review the multiple choice options one of my students offered this gem of wisdom: "If they'd just read the Bible they'd get a clue; God spoke it into existence." My classroom, filled with students from good rural conservative homes, was silent. "You know I don't say anything for or against religion in my classroom," I began. "We do science; I leave the religion to you and your families." Turning to the young man, I continued, "I do want, though, to share an observation on why you are a Bible-believing Christian. I'm sure there are many reasons, but among them is the coincidence that you were born into it. If you had been born in Iraq, you'd be a devout young Muslim. In India, a Hindu; in Israel, a Jew. In Japan, a Buddhist. Right?" He nodded.

I went on to point out that our religious differences, sometimes the backdrop to cultural mistrust, conflict, and war, depend tremendously on the coincidence of our birth. Each of those various religions will continue to exist because religious belief is not subject to independent verification of evidence; it is a thing of the heart. Scientists in all those different cultures can explore, experiment, challenge each other's theories, and end up in independently verified consensus. I wrapped up that brief monologue with, "To me, and I know this isn't for everyone, my most deeply held 'belief' has to be in second place to hard evidence, even if I don't like the evidence. More importantly, any beliefs I choose or manage to hang on to need to be held with a humility that allows me to acknowledge that others around the world may be just as 'right' as I am."

A teachers' aid who for several years had endured my methodical teaching of evolution chided me later saying, "Science is just your chosen religion." We discussed that proposition at length. A devout Christian woman who walked her talk, she enjoyed the benefit of my respect; and I suppose because she knew I came from a devout Christian background, knew and stuck to the facts, and didn't push atheism, I enjoyed the benefit of her respect. In the end I was able to get her somewhat reluctant acknowledgment of a **key difference between science and religion**. Religion of any type that we know of has a set of assertions that it sticks with; its emphasis is on its conclusions (including the modern assertion that it is the 'relationship' that matters). Science has a process it sticks with; science willingly changes conclusions when the process and resulting evidence indicate the conclusion should be changed. Science isn't dogma, it's an open-minded search to understand, and it focuses on explanations of natural processes, things that can be tested. That necessarily means we don't stop short with, "Oh, that must be supernatural."

The important thing here is to recognize the different starting points that people come from. We could call this bias. It's the set of lenses, presuppositions, through which we filter information. Consider the following: We may not like it, but today's world is increasingly integrated in a multitude of ways; we are indeed a global village. Living constructively as part of that village requires a high level of insightful and foresightful decision-making on the part of nations, leaders, and citizens. Doing this on a global level requires a lot of 'information consumption and processing.' Being a consumer of information in an age of intense and instant media coverage calls for being not only aware and concerned, it calls for being to a great degree an independent analyst of, and a critical thinker about, the information with which we are swamped. Consider for a moment the outright twisting or subtle spinning of information, and this need is magnified.

A key part to becoming a critical analyst of the information we are fed is learning to recognize bias. Learning to recognize bias in others starts with learning to recognize it in oneself. The initial temptation is to say "Me? I'm not biased. I happen to see things clearly. I'm a person of conviction." But in actual fact we each do start out with certain assumptions. Twenty-some years ago one of my biases was, "The Bible is the clearest explanation of our state of affairs on earth and our place in the universe." I filtered other information through that lens first. Some information/facts got thrown out because they didn't fit through my filter.

I was in for some rough sailing though, because some of my other biases set me up for internal conflict. I also had the bias that, "Right understanding should ultimately match up with the bulk of the verifiable evidence when you pay careful attention to detail and keep the big picture in mind (see the forest **and** the trees)." After a few years of some confusion, and after I had time to reflect on what I learned in Lebanon and Rwanda, I came up with a new bias. "When there is a conflict between what my preferred beliefs are and what verifiable evidence says, I'm going to require myself to let the evidence win and my preferred beliefs lose." Now some previous beliefs have been thrown out because they don't fit my new filter. At least this way I'm being more honest with myself and with the evidence. For a more complete look at my biases check Appendix A for a little section titled "I Hold These Truths to be Self-evident."

When crossing the paths of the numerous conservative church-going believers with whom I still have occasional contact, I have learned to use another conscious filter. If these individuals seem to have an appropriate humility to their beliefs and a respect for religious freedom, and the implied respect for the equal legitimacy of others' beliefs, I tread very gently and avoid rocking their boat. On the other hand, when I detect a cocky certainty that "our beliefs are the only true way," I begin to probe. It's easy to ask troubling questions. Sometimes a few scattered individuals even seem to begin to think deeply in search of real understanding.

Academics have long looked suspiciously at religion; it is time that we everyday-folk look in the mirror and acknowledge that it's a distinct possibility, like it or not, that there is no God. Even if we take the side that says, "Well, it isn't impossible – there could be a God, so I choose to believe," let's at least acknowledge that since no tradition about God does a good job of matching up with the verifiable evidence on earth and in the universe, then 'god' must be very different than any of us have imagined. That ought to help us take our chosen tradition about God with considerably more humility, and thus be more open to other cultures and their traditions.

Religion may not be a placebo, on the other hand it very well might be. It can't actually be demonstrated conclusively to everyone's satisfaction. On that we each make a choice, consciously or not. Some choose to believe what they want to believe, while others choose to accept what the verifiable evidence suggests. If one wants to believe in God, who is to argue with it? But, let's not allow a simple choice of belief and accompanying loyalty to it to become the basis of much more practical decisions that really do affect the stability of human culture, earth's ecological balance, or our nation's economic stability. In fact, there may not be any supernatural solutions to problems we've made or made worse. Yes, Jesus Christ may or may not return to solve our problems. Further, God's 'Will' is open to each culture's and each individual's interpretation. So, let's be responsible and farsighted in using our ability to logically solve our problems before we destroy ourselves or our earth.

Some will read a statement like "Some choose to believe what they want to believe, while others choose to accept what the verifiable evidence suggests" and think something like "The arrogant bastard!" Thus I feel compelled to clarify. I am no genius, and I don't think of myself as one. It is not that my thinking is superior, but it is different than the current majority, though fortunately I am far from alone. The difference can't be measured in IQ points; it can be measured in level of objectivity. Those who have learned to think this way are willing to sacrifice what they would prefer to believe in favor of what actually measures up to analysis. Please remember, I grew up on and loved the paintings and stories of Adam and Eve in the Garden of Eden, of Noah's ark and the animals coming in two-by-two, of angels ascending and descending Jacob's ladder, and of Jesus rising from the tomb, and walking on water. I loved all those stories. I haven't changed to my current thinking because I wanted to. I've changed because open, honest, objective analysis has compelled me to. I expect more of myself and all of us in an educated and privileged society than I do of an illiterate villager in some poverty-ridden corner of the world. The beliefs they inherit are about all they have, so of course they hold on to them without further thought, and sometimes with blind ferocity. We must take a tough, deep, thorough, and painfully honest look at how our tendency to cling loyally to any and all of our clan's positions, religious, political, or ecological, leads us to shortsighted decisions. We can and must do better.

At the gut level there will be a variety of responses to these thoughts. Some, like the six-year-old whose sibling just revealed the truth about Santa, will huff and stomp away yelling "You're wrong! Santa's still real!" Another of the same age may say "I already knew that." Still another may say "So? It's fun to believe." What's important is that they be able to get on with real life without making shortsighted and ill-informed choices.

At the risk of redundancy, let me reiterate. This is **not** a call on believers to quit believing. It is a call on believers to take their stewardship of planet earth and their fellow humans seriously, practically, now, and permanently. Yes, to acknowledge that: accepting or ignoring a world of ridiculous inequity with regions of abject poverty stuck in hopelessness is to accept a world which will become progressively less stable. To acknowledge that: our myopic preoccupation with economic growth and the personal accumulation of wealth while ignoring deteriorating ecosystems locally and globally is to invite disaster on our descendants.

The secular humanist's doubts about 'God', should his doubts turn out to be wrong, won't have hurt the believer's eternity. But the believer who lets his faith keep him from action, should he turn out to be wrong about 'God' rescuing us, will have hurt the quality of life on earth for those around him – especially that of future generations. And if that believer's faith is held without the humility of acknowledging that other faiths are equally legitimate, the temptation toward cultural conflict with the notion that "God is on our side" gets much more insidious.

If we cultivate the tendency to question and openly analyze all sides to an argument, even our own clan's positions, we'll find ourselves having overcome the lion's share of the problems with blind loyalty. When enough of us have cultivated that habit in ourselves and helped it begin to take root in our fellow-citizens, we won't have to wait for politicians to lead. We, the people, will lead because we will choose leaders who 'get' this.

Interestingly, while many parts of this book focus on actual policy-making processes and thinking, what is at the heart of it is the goal of having an educated and thinking citizenry take a more active role in their democracy. This chapter necessarily must have no policy impact. It would be as much a disaster to have government making any policy against religion as it would to have government endorsing religion in any form. The impact of this chapter is hopefully to shift away from shortsighted decisions premised on there being a final supernatural solution to our problems, and toward farsighted decisions that take responsibility for the results of our actions.

One of the practical changes that this shift in thinking and decision-making will bring is that we will choose different types of leaders than we sometimes have in the past. This type of leader wouldn't fall for ill-founded cultural conflicts or outright wars because they won't have the backdrop thoughts of "the real solutions being supernatural," or of "God working out His will through this fight," or "I'm in office because it is God's will, so what I happen to think must be part of this higher authority." And they won't blindly stick to their guns in the face of contrary evidence because they won't have the habit of being married to their pre-set conclusions. They'll have at least somewhat of a tendency to focus on process (thoroughness and objectivity of information gathering, and open and careful analysis), and be open to changing conclusions as the evidence dictates. And eventually we will be ready and able to genuinely listen, without emotionally rebelling, to a leader who advocates the necessary tough choices and action even over various warm-fuzzies of reassurance. Wow, what a world it could be – but we, the people, better have the courage to break from prior rigidly-fixed mindsets and have the commitment-to-action to lead, to break new ground.

Section II:
The Immediate & Long-term War Against Terrorism

Chapter 3.

Beyond "I Want It Now":
The Battle vs. the War

Simple Truth # 3. We bear significant responsibility for the growth of large-scale terrorism.

This truth isn't about beating ourselves up like an abused wife finding ways to blame herself. It is simply about analyzing things to gain insight and ultimately bring terrorism to an end. First of all, we need to make a fine but significant distinction. I do NOT believe that terrorism is justified. We can though, seek to understand even wholly unjustified behavior. Studies of horrific crimes and child abuse regularly seek to understand the unjustifiable.

When various types of sociopaths arise, society doesn't necessarily need to seek out reasons why. David Koresh (the Branch Davidian leader in Waco, Texas, 1993), Jim Jones (of Jonestown, Guyana, 1978), and Timothy McVeigh (of Oklahoma City, Oklahoma, 1995) were crazy people who did terrible things, but we as a society did not need to soul-search for what was behind their craziness. Why not? Because they didn't succeed in getting tens of thousands of people to join them in an openly violent conquest against innocent civilians.

Osama bin Laden is crazy too. The trouble is, his craziness isn't nearly as easy to dismiss because his cause has attracted legions. Why has he attracted a large, committed, and self-sacrificing following that reaches far beyond the poor and disenfranchised? This is a question we must seek to answer. And in seeking to answer this question, we must be vigilant in not simply reaffirming our prior beliefs; we must be open to actual evidence, and do our best to honestly analyze it.

A sports analogy might be useful before getting into the heart of the matter. As we know, in baseball they differentiate between earned and unearned runs. The difference between earned and unearned runs takes on added importance if you look at earned and unearned enemies. Some people are going to hate you and be your enemies even if you've done nothing to earn their hatred. They are your unearned enemies, and, in contrast to baseball, you have to accept that you'll have some. (And you better be ready to fight them and win.) On the other hand are your earned enemies, and you'd certainly be smart to figure out what you've been doing, probably unintentionally and unwittingly, to earn them. Then you can fix it, end up with a fraction of the enemies, and have a much better chance of winning the game.

So back to our question of what has made extremist/radical Islam grow from a small fragment to what it is today. Have we inadvertently been adding earned enemies to our unearned ones? Imagine for a moment that we all live in one big peculiar city that has its own form of order. Neighborhoods are ruled by organized and rather civil gangs. They don't exist to do trade in illicit drugs; they **are** the law enforcement agents, and to a great degree they cooperate across most neighborhoods. The leader of the main gang resembles Mike Tyson in his prime, and differences are settled in arranged bouts inside a regulation boxing ring. Now you and I happen to have some major beefs with the way this Tyson-like enforcer runs our lives. We can't get decent jobs, our kids don't get quality schooling, we can't leave, our wives live in fear, and we face constant humiliation. When we've brought up our grievances, the reply always includes references to settling our differences in the ring. Now you and I might be in good shape and decent athletes, but getting in the ring for a "fair fight" with Mike Tyson in his prime would be rather like committing suicide.

So when we stand no chance of winning a fair fight, what do we do? Well, we're going to resort to "unfair" techniques. True, if we have discerning character, we'll try to catch this enforcer himself in a dark alley with our baseball bats, and we'll leave the innocent members of his family alone.

As a young man working in Lebanon in 1980-81, I had occasion to witness war and peace, prosperity and poverty, hope and despair, and a depth of religious conviction (of several types) that made true believers willing to commit acts of violence. I saw a kind of clan mentality in action. Before I left the Middle East, I took a little time to travel in Jordan and Israel. During all of this, I engaged anyone with whom I could communicate in conversation. I asked a lot of questions, and did a lot of listening.

Back in America a year later I called in to talk with Larry King and his guest-expert on the Middle East. Among the things I said to them was something like, "The Middle East doesn't stand a chance for peace until and unless the Palestinian people have a legitimate and respected homeland." Both Larry and his guest concurred. Still a year after that, while teaching in a suburb of Los Angeles, I contacted representatives of both the Jewish and Palestinian communities to make presentations and lead discussion in my social studies class. Needless to say, it's a difficult issue.

I don't pretend for one second that the Palestinian homeland issue is the only thing that is behind al-Qaida's recruiting ability, but it has been a long-standing thorn in the side of Muslims and Arabs, and is a significant contributing factor. The point for the moment is that we have been Israel's enforcer, we have given them largely unquestioning and one-sided support. The broad perception in the Muslim/Arab world is that we are not even-handed in our handling of issues that affect them. (We all know that there are huge numbers of Muslims who are not Arab, and a fair number of Arabs who are not Muslim. I use the "/" symbol to mean "both" populations, not that they are the same.) Unable to step in the ring and win a fair fight with Israel and us, they resorted to unfair and unethical techniques, to terrorism. One can wish that they would have focused their surprise tactics on military targets (something that might actually have helped their cause), but they haven't. It doesn't make it right; it is dead wrong to attack innocent and uninvolved civilians. But it shouldn't be completely unbelievable that when you corner something in desperate circumstances, be they human or animal, they might react in violent desperation. We would do well at this point to remember that relatively desperate circumstances reach well beyond Palestinian refugee camps to the disenfranchised or extremely frustrated in cities like Cairo and Damascus.

I will deal more with Israel and with what religious conflict adds to terrorism in a later chapter, but for now let me reassure anyone inclined to think otherwise that I believe Israel has a right to exist. The world's support in the creation of Israel in the aftermath of the Holocaust was justified. But some aspects of that creation led to wronging another people, and two wrongs don't make a right.

The real issue here and now is that we have to do more than fight today's terrorists. We have to figure out what drives their recruiting of tomorrow's terrorists, and we have to have the guts to begin to do something about it. In order to fully reveal Osama bin Laden's craziness for what it is, we have to deprive him of the few legitimate issues he mixes in with his irrational agenda. There really are millions of civil, right-thinking Muslims/Arabs. We want to help isolate al-Qaida as the extremists they are; instead our foreign policy during the George W. Bush era ended up isolating us.

At times it is too easy for us in the west to wonder where the civil, right-thinking Muslims are. The TV images we see naturally don't focus on them, and unless you've lived among them, assuming that moderates almost don't exist can creep into our beliefs. It is simply an exaggerated case of the same general phenomenon we suffer here. Those in the middle, the majority, get drowned out by the hard-liners. The challenge there, as here, is to have the middle step up and speak up. Let us not lose focus though by being side-tracked to what we expect them to do. That's a challenge they must deal with, and one I address directly at the end of the next chapter. We must stay focused right now on what we have been doing, are doing, and can do.

The Palestinian issue is an old recruiting tool, and our invasion and occupation of Iraq is a new one. After 9-11, the world at large, including significant portions of the Muslim/Arab world, was with us. We had broad and even overwhelming support in going into Afghanistan to oust the Taliban and get al-Qaida. At that point moderate Muslims (the majority), despite the long-standing Palestinian issue and perhaps other lesser issues, weren't attracted to al-Qaida. As we began to rattle our sword over

Iraq, that began to change. If our own allies were distancing themselves from us, what do you think your average Arab/Muslim (who while not hating us, did hold us in mistrust and suspicion) was doing? When we could have continued to build our team and isolate al-Qaida, our obvious plans to invade Iraq (premised on reasons even our allies doubted) actually ended up isolating ourselves and building al-Qaida's team.

Am I saying Saddam Hussein was a good guy? No way! But was our leadership taking the time and using insight to see the long run? Equally, no way! The really sad thing is that there were people within ear-shot of President Bush who were warning him of this folly, but he had very selective hearing. There is a critical difference between truly imminent threat and a regime we happen to intensely dislike and mistrust.

Another unfortunate thing about our invasion of Iraq and the predictable (and predicted) difficulties it has brought is that we, the American population, passed on a chance to show the world, and moderate Muslims in particular, that we didn't agree with the invasion. When someone demonstrates their close-mindedness and lack of foreign policy insight and foresight on the job, it is sad when we let fear (of unknown leadership and of then fresh al-Qaida threats) keep us from sending the world a worth-while message. In the 2004 election our votes could have said, "We were wrong to let this man take us there." The ever-increasing number of middle-Americans who wish they had said that then, said it in the election of 2006, and vigorously reinforced it in the election of 2008. We, the people, have just begun to seriously correct a major al-Qaida recruiting tool.

With only a fairly short history of our involvement in Iraq to analyze, there seems to be conflicting information on Iraq. On one hand there is the Downing Street memo's intimation that the Bush Administration was simply committed to having this fight. On the other hand are the conclusions of the 9-11 commission which focused more on what to do now rather than what we need to learn about how we got there. The long run will be much clearer. There are memoirs yet to be written which will continue to reveal a president obsessed early on with Iraq, and just looking for the right excuse. While talking about the dangers of Iraq and weapons of mass destruction and then acting on it, Mr. Bush succeeded in enlarging al-Qaida's recruiting base, thus making it not less but more likely that one day we may well face the horrors of a nuclear flash over a city full of civilians.

It is an interesting sidelight to our fight against terrorism to note how our invasion of Iraq has also affected our relations with established regimes like Iran. We must keep the broad context in mind. For at least a decade prior to our invasion of Iraq, the relatively "secular" middle in Iran was growing in numbers and influence, and the hardliners were being weakened. When we invaded Afghanistan with the overwhelming support of the world at large, most in Iran didn't object even though the shared border and close American presence probably stirred some hardliners.

Then we planned and executed our invasion of Iraq. Now our presence in Afghanistan and Iraq, and our influence in Pakistan nearly surrounded Iran. It is no doubt far too easy for us to say something like, "So what? We're the good guys. What do they have to worry about?" But if you are a hardliner in Iran, you now have more evidence to support your talk of America's material imperialism, injustice, or whatever fear-mongering theme you choose. And if you were one of the once growing moderates in Iran, you are likely driven either toward radical positions or into silence.

In the tough situation we find ourselves in with regard

to how to handle Iran, we can only wish we still had the global political capital we had after 9-11 but before invading Iraq. If we had that capital, not only would we be in a much stronger position to deal with them, but **more significantly, we quite likely wouldn't be in a confrontational situation at all because the radicals wouldn't even be in power there**. We, by poorly thought through strategic decisions, drove them back from growing moderate influence into the arms of waiting radicals. It really shouldn't surprise us when our surrounding an independent state with our military power results in that state becoming more confrontational and less cooperative.

Skepticism of generalizations is a good thing, and one can easily check on the validity of the idea that *our* actions put the current radicals in power in Iran. Although I still hope to minimize the interruption of citations, the details here necessitate it; you can check out the following facts on the ups and downs of recent and current Iranian leadership in a broad array of sources beginning with GlobalSecurity. org. I independently bring your attention to the timely connections between our actions and events there.

Reformist President Mohammed Khatami was elected in 1997 and re-elected in June of 2001. One of his first acts was to dismiss a man named Mahmoud Ahmadinejad from his regional governorship of Ardabil province in 1997. Ahmadinejad went quietly back to being an engineering professor. In October of 2001 we invaded Afghanistan, and nothing changed in Iran. Then in March of 2003, a year a half later, we invaded Iraq and began to topple Saddam Hussein. The results: five months after we invaded Iraq, the radical current President of Iran, Ahmadinejad was appointed Mayor of Tehran, the capital city. And less than two years later, this man who had been demoted from his regional governorship in '97, was now apparently 'electable' because he did win the presidency.

We don't like dealing with this guy, and who would? But who are the geniuses who made him electable? Have you read any parts of the "Project for the New American Century"? You should. Signed by the likes of Dick Cheney, Donald Rumsfeld, and Jeb Bush, you run into phrases like "American military supremacy" and America's need to "assert its primacy in world politics." Sounds fine from here; but **honestly** imagine you're a Swede, Indonesian, Nigerian, Venezuelan, or an Iranian! Much more than our words though, actions like our excuse-laden invasion of a sovereign country do shift people against us. When our actions corner or surround people, and our words make them question our motives, do we really expect a cooperative response?

No, I don't have a crystal ball and didn't predict the details of Ahmadinejad's rise, but many of us predicted that our unjustified invasion of Iraq would lead to a general shift toward empowering radicals in Muslim countries. We actually chose the leaders who decided invading Iraq was a good idea; yes, we made our bed, and of course we don't like lying in it. There's a lesson here somewhere.

The discussion of whether or not President Bush outright lied to us in making the case for invading Iraq was at one point too hot for objective discussion. I have sometimes thought that the overall evidence doesn't point to deliberate, planned deception. Rather, we elected a man who never showed any natural tendency to be introspective about his own motives and no habit of careful analysis of possible realities beyond what he happened to believe. To compound matters, he never tried to correct for what he didn't see as a weak spot. He proudly proclaimed that he believes *what* he believes; but he appeared to have never thought of and certainly never proclaimed *how* he figures things out. To one degree or another we all share the tendency to reach the conclusions we want before we fully digest the evidence. Then we stick with those conclusions, political or religious, for the rest of our lives. The more we can be aware of and fight that temptation, the more reliable both our thought processes and our conclusions.

The difference between decisions, personal or national, made based on what we want to believe (our ideology) versus those based on objective analysis of evidence is of vital importance. One of the single greatest areas of importance bears directly on whether we manage to narrow the current conflict or let it mushroom out of control.

Various congregations have invited speakers whose message seems to be "All Muslims have the goal of taking over the world for Allah." Under attack as we are, some seem to *want* to believe that; they sit and nod their heads while receiving a message from someone who claims to have insight, telling them what they already believe.

Think about this for a second. Here we are in a society where the least educated among us in general have completed most or all of high school. They have had at least one class in world history, in logical thinking through geometry, in the scientific method and valid conclusions, and in at least rudimentary aspects of literary analysis, including elementary aspects of recognizing bias. The more educated among us have had even more opportunity to see the world broadly and objectively. **If we, a relatively well-educated culture, are still inclined to listen to extremists among us who beat drums of fear, who broadly portray the whole Muslim culture as evil and violent, what in the world do we expect of them?**

Hands down, despite good numbers of them being highly educated, the masses there have not had as much opportunity for basic education. They have their own extremists beating the drums of fear and hatred. **Are they somehow going to be less susceptible to believing ideologically driven nonsense about us?**

If we don't step up to the plate and rationally and calmly confront our own ideologues (be they top politicians, fellow church members, or co-workers) who simply spout what they happen to believe, we will be guilty of having let the conflict unnecessarily and tragically broaden. We **must** meet this challenge. We can re-narrow the conflict.

We must consciously note the difference between fighting with intensity and winning skirmishes here and there while generating more long-term enemies vs. actually looking at our actions and attitudes from the long-term perspective, and finding a way to not only fight today's terrorists but to reduce their appeal and put tomorrow's terrorists in a steady decline.

That difference, between winning the moment's battle vs. focusing on the long-term war, is something I've become convinced not enough of us really think about. While we can't look forward to a near-future, specific day of victory against terrorism, we can work toward minimizing it to the point where we will have restored a world with some basic assurance of security and normalcy.

The question is essentially whether or not we will let this struggle continue to broaden in terms of it involving nearly whole cultures and regions, or whether we can re-narrow the conflict to the extremist radicals who started it. This is a critical difference at this juncture.

If we just fight and even win specific battles with terrorists, but don't narrow the conflict to the point of eventually being able to win this very different 'war,' the future, measured from a few years to multiple generations, could easily degenerate into a modern repeat of the Dark Ages.

This time around though, the crusades wouldn't kill just scattered thousands of involved volunteers. With weapons of mass destruction, modern crusades could not only kill millions, but could disrupt or destroy so many aspects of modern society and technology that we could be set back millennia – perhaps never again to arrive at our current potential.

If you still find yourself tempted to follow leaders "of strong conviction," who really believe what they believe, allow me to point out that the ultimate in leaders with a depth of faith and conviction is Osama bin Laden. He never pauses in self-analysis or reflection of what beyond his belief system might make good sense. He doesn't subject his preferred beliefs to the possible modifications that objectively verifiable evidence might bring. He sticks to his guns. Is that the kind of leadership we want to follow, is that how we ourselves want to sort out life? If we can't resist the temptation to give our chosen beliefs priority over objectively verifiable evidence, we're in for a world of hurt because this conflict will broaden, deepen, and intensify.

The flip-side to being firmly set in our preferred beliefs without regard for real verifiable evidence is very liberating and allows us to avoid unnecessary conflict. We will discuss this further in the next chapter.

Several weeks before we invaded Iraq I listened in as some of my students discussed the apparently up-coming invasion. Noticing me listening and knowing that I had a tendency to see things from a different perspective, a couple of these young rural Republicans-in-the-making challenged me to join in and say something. I gave them this illustration: Imagine our school has a total stud athlete. He's bigger, stronger, faster, and has great coordination and vision; he's by far the best athlete our school has ever had. Now imagine that one of the rival schools in our league has the same kind of stud. They're alike except for attitude. One of them swaggers down the hall. On the field or court his approach is "Just gimmie the ball."

The other guy walks with humility that almost hides his strength. On the field or court he loves the "assist." Yes, you can count on him at crunch time if you need him, but he loves sharing the load and the glory with his teammates. Now, which guy is more likely to develop enemies? And which guy's teammates are more likely to stick with him should he really need them? With a nod, most of my students acknowledged that they got it. We have allies, teammates. We can leave them feeling like their input doesn't matter, or we can be a genuine team player. My students also saw that our attitude, perceived even if not always real, of swaggering around the globe doing it our way, no matter what, only makes more people pass the critical balance point from mistrusting us to hating us. We lend our real enemies a stronger recruiting base and make it more likely we'll meet with more proverbial baseball bats in dark alleys.

What now? It's extremely tough. In late 2005 I wrote the following: I know I'll disappoint some in this, but I am not in favor of withdrawing the troops now, or at any artificially imposed date. To quit while chaos reigns in Iraq would only embolden today's terrorists and add the momentum of a win to their future recruiting. I don't think George Bush would have the honesty and courage to personally step up and say, "I was wrong to push for this war, but I'm not going to commit a second wrong to try to make a right. We can't leave prematurely. We must stay until we've helped the Iraqi people get their feet on solid ground." (Although limited admissions of errors like prisoner abuse, civilian casualties, inflammatory talk, and underestimating the power of instant information are small steps in the right direction, they don't get close to "I was wrong to push for this war.") I believe it would be helpful though if someone reasonably high in the State Department articulated something along those lines because it would actually help wrap things up. We'd be less "suspect" of having ulterior motives.

Is it possible that things will continue to get worse over there? Unfortunately, yes. Could we reach a point reminiscent of the last helicopters lifting off the embassy roof in Saigon? Again, yes. We must though, have the guts, courage, and willingness to sacrifice to make every effort to ensure that doesn't happen. How will we know if we reach the point of truly having lost? I don't know, and fervently hope we never find out. If that ever happens, during the decades in which terrorism will be worse, rather than simply pointing fingers back at Bush, Cheney, Rove, and Rumsfeld, I hope we have the honesty and guts to accept our own role in the whole mess. We, regular citizens across America, passively let our country be led by short-sighted leaders who lacked insight into the complexity of other cultures and our real and perceived role in the world; we let our beliefs out-weigh rational analysis of actual evidence... we let the conflict broaden. This isn't about assigning blame, it is simply about learning from experience. The real lesson may be that we all have to speak up and do whatever it takes to get the ear of our leaders. Even if we ultimately succeed in getting Iraq to stability and avoiding the surge of terrorism that losing could bring, the same lesson is there!

No doubt there are some who immediately write off talk of fixing what we've done or are doing that contributes to terrorism's growth as simply naïve. Well, let's remind ourselves of what naïveté involves. It is being unaware of basic realities that should be known at certain developmental levels. Thus the "hawk" thinks that it is naïve to analyze and fix our role in terror's existence and growth because he supposes that it ignores the basic reality that there are genuine bad-guy crazies who must be fought. Note though, that he is himself being naïve because he is ignoring the basic reality that you actually can broaden your enemy's long-term appeal by broadening the conflict to include whole cultures and religions, and by being go-it-alone... my way or the highway.

Now, in 2010, because circumstances appear to have changed significantly, I've modified my position. Few would debate that things are actually much better in Iraq; fortunately there seems to be actual non-spun evidence that gives cause for hope. Still, most don't foresee a real end to our involvement there in the better part of a decade or more! That's a frightening admission. **If** our being there simply fuels the insurgent fire, and allows the Sunni and Shia to continue their sectarian battles without facing the reality that they must *either* agree to cohabit and constructively manage their united county *or* they are in fact dooming themselves to unending violence, **then** we might as well say we're done and pull off the best exit we can. It is about time to say "We're done. We can only hope that you can bring yourselves to peace and reconstruction." Why spend more lives? Really! On the other hand, **if** the Sunni, Shia, and Kurds really step up to living together and working out unity, **then** we can agree to stay and help rebuild but not referee, for considerably longer.

In any case, while it may be *pressing* for our nation to decide what to do at any particular point in time, the "now" of the moment, the really *important* thing is to learn the big lessons. On a shallow level, ideologues make attractive leaders; their very intensity of belief gathers followers. But those ideologues are quick to get into unnecessary fights. We, the people, need to get past that shallow attraction, and learn to choose leaders who emphasize in word and action "how" they think and figure things out, not simply "what" they happen to believe. Many of us hope that the election of Barack Obama represents the beginning of our learning, and that he will continue to put into practice what appears so far to be an un-Bush-like respect for the thinking process over fixed belief and permanent conclusions.

There will continue to be discussions of how we've made various errors in planning and managing the war in Iraq, but they all fail to go back and recognize the basic reality that **there is no right way to fight the wrong war**, and that we as a society must learn the difference between leaders with strong beliefs (ideology) and leaders with the courage to think things through, to analyze and learn. For a thorough look at the rightness or wrongness of the Iraq war, see Chapter 6; for a thorough look at choosing leadership, see Chapter 5.

Remember the baseball analogy? We have got to get better at fighting our unearned enemies while not gathering new earned enemies. If we can succeed at limiting ourselves to unearned enemies, at re-narrowing the conflict, we will indeed stand a much better chance of winning this war against terrorism.

Chapter 4.

"My" Better Angels:
The Role of Religion in This War

If these times weren't extraordinary, I wouldn't be speaking out on our role in terrorism and I certainly wouldn't be saying anything about anyone's religious beliefs. But as illustrated earlier, these are not normal times. The potential for large-scale disaster if we let ourselves fall into a modern version of the crusades-of-old is simply too great. It is not an accident that I refer to the historical Crusades. Those were cultural wars, ostensibly fought for religious reasons. Kings and sultans invoked the name of God, then generals marshaled their volunteers in the name of God, and on both sides those volunteers died for, and killed for, their beliefs in their God.

Today we have religious fundamentalists of the Islamic variety behind terrorism. They invoke the name of God and are willing to die and to kill. Amazingly, many in our educated modern country respond as if they believe that the best response to one type of religious extremism is to develop and strengthen our own brand of religious extremism. Citizens and political leaders, soldiers and pastors can be heard invoking the name of God in our battle with terrorists. Can we think for a moment that declaring God to be on our side makes it so? In actuality, mimicking our enemies and declaring God to be on 'our' side may simply give them more motivation to prove us dead wrong.

I go into a number of simple truths related to religion with great reluctance. I think of religious belief as near and dear to the heart, and your choice of religious belief doesn't have to answer to my rationale. But in America today there is a serious effort to force the beliefs of Evangelical Christendom into public policy – into domestic law via the legislature and the courts, and during the Bush II administration even into foreign policy. Because this impacts the scale of the battle, drawing in whole cultures and countries instead of leaving fundamentalists isolated, I cannot withhold comment.

I know that on a topic as sensitive and personal as this, some will inevitably be offended. If you happen to be a "true believer" of some type, I hope your idea of God includes forgiveness and patience, because you may find that you need both to get through some of this. If you persevere, I think some of you will be persuaded by the evidence and good sense I offer. True die-hards will never be convinced, and that's okay. It is my hope though that I do convince here-to-fore too-silent middle-Americans that we cannot afford to stay silent and let ourselves be dragged into a religion-dominated society and religiously driven wars.

Simple Truths
4. Muslim fundamentalists are a serious impediment to peace.

Duh! No real discussion needed here. But in case some of the non-extremist Muslims of the world wind up reading this, it is you more than anyone else who can effectively isolate your extremists and clear your own good name. For your community's sake, and for the sake of the future of the human race, step up and work to isolate extremists. More on this theme later.

5. Jewish fundamentalists are a serious impediment to peace.

Not so obvious to some, this may merit some discussion. There are secular Jews around the world. I've met and had discussions with some in Israel and in America. It is my distinct impression that they have reasonable expectations, a willingness to compromise with Palestinians, and a desire to live and let live in peace.

There are also fundamentalist Jews around the world. I've also met and had discussions with some of them. They've been honest in expressing their clear belief of their place in the world. They are Jews, God's chosen people, the apple of His eye. The rest of us are Gentiles, to be tolerated at best. It's not our fault; it's just how it is.

Their claims to special status and to land are relatively easy for most people to shrug off as nonsense or rationalize as "conditional promises." But if your historical land is the same piece as theirs, as is the case with the Palestinians, shrugging is not so easy. For a couple generations now you have had to deal with settlements and fundamentalist settlers occupying progressively greater portions of what had been yours. If secular, moderate Jews had been in firm control of their politics, they would have been able to implement policies which the Palestinian people, the majority of whom are not radicals, would have found acceptable.

6. Christian fundamentalists are a serious impediment to peace.

Now wait a minute some may say. This is not so easy, and so may require significant discussion. Along the way we will note a number of sub-set simple truths.

An increase in prayer, both public and private, was a very understandable reaction to 9-11. On that day we came under attack, and wherever we were, we felt that visceral fear; indeed, there are almost "No atheists in fox-holes." But various religious and political leaders have used that initial primal fear and the subsequent lasting feeling of insecurity to magnify our cultural differences. Rather than think analytically, to look objectively at evidence history can offer us, too many leaders have sought followers who are blindly willing to simply strengthen their belief systems. Too many have been willing to embrace the idea that "God" is on any side in a war, and since "He must be on our side," all of the believers in other "false" religions must be wrong and must be fought as a whole group.

The Arab/Muslim world accesses our media. Those hearing and reading these comments by far-right talking heads and Christian extremists are not unaffected. When they see that they have been painted negatively with a very broad brush, their reaction is naturally to assume that these radical statements reflect the American majority opinion. Thus they in turn paint us with a very broad brush. And so the cycle goes. Fairly quickly you can go from narrow, albeit strong, ideological differences to broad cultural conflict, to having whole countries a lot closer to all-out war. How quickly this happens depends to a great degree on the relative degree of education vs. primitiveness of the countries in question.

This brings us to a number of subset simple truths.

#6a. The more primitive the society, the less likely they are to question their own basic religious beliefs.

#6b. The more educated the society, the more they should be able to acknowledge that different religious

views are equally legitimate, and that religion isn't subject to verification of objective facts.

I've listened more than once to good Christians comment on the primitiveness of cultures and societies where voters base their decisions on the clan, ethnic group, or religious affiliation of the candidates. It's ironic then when those same Christians state their position on a political race or issue here in America with words like, "Because he/she is a born again Christian," or, "That's the Christian position."

#6c. It took Christianity multiple centuries to reach the point of going through the Renaissance and developing the historical-critical method. We should expect it is going to take Muslims a while to broaden their willingness to critically analyze their own texts, beliefs, and the degree of connection between religion and politics.

This puts the onus on us to be more patient with them than we can expect them to be with us. I must stress though, I'm not talking of patience with terrorism. We must fight that, not only with strength, but with wisdom. Rather, I'm pointing to patience with little irritations like their narrow definition of truth and them calling the West infidels. That doesn't need to hurt us, and we certainly don't need to retort with similar name-calling.

I know some who still genuinely feel that they are not being paranoid in fearing that Muslims as a whole are out to get us, to conquer the world. I would simply point out that while that is the aim of radical fundamentalist Muslims, radical fundamentalists of any kind have never shown an ability to stay unified. Look at your own Christian denomination or even local congregation. The more inflexibly some assertive subgroup holds their beliefs, the more likely they are to fracture from within. We don't have to fear a unified Muslim attack, unless it is we who unify them with our own irrational attacks. Fundamentalists can't keep a united front, or even a united core.

In any case, the best long-term way to prevent a global take-over by any fundamentalist group is through promoting real education and broad economic engagement. Real education, not indoctrination, promotes independent and analytical thinking, which is the very antidote to fundamentalism. And economic engagement that involves infinitely more than exploiting mineral wealth promotes the development of a real middle class. Both of these are prerequisites to lasting democracy; trying to do democracy first isn't likely to work for a multitude of reasons. (One of the books which I highly recommend and which so thoroughly makes the point I have simplified here is *The Future of Freedom*, by Fareed Zakaria. It is thought provoking and deep, and very worth your time.)

Back to the immediate need for our calm patience with the broad Muslim culture. While narrowly and intensely fighting terrorism, it is worthwhile remembering that the answer to them declaring their very nationhood and form of governance to be based on one religion doesn't need to be that we declare ourselves to be a nation based on another religion.

7. America is a secular nation, not a Christian one.

This is a hot button, and if it weren't for the definite movement trying to impose the opposite I wouldn't touch it; but we middle-Americans must stand up or get railroaded.

Some relatively recent events and trends can help make this discussion less dry and abstract and become much more real and practical. Some may remember "Justice Sunday." That huge televised meeting in Louisville, held in April of 2005, seemed intended to galvanize the true-believer Christians among us into supporting various aspects of making Christian values into the law of the land. That meeting got a lot of attention.

At almost the same time several pastors in my hometown held a "Celebration of All Faiths." A half-dozen people attended. Surprising? No, but why not? Why indeed would two meetings, both on religious themes and both organized by religious people, draw such different levels of interest? The leaders of the first meeting focused on points that divide us, while the leaders of the second meeting focused on issues that unite us. But should it begin to raise our concerns when unity draws a yawn but divisiveness draws a crowd? I trust the answer is obvious. The point for the moment is that if we don't carefully watch ourselves, we are easy prey to divisive issues and divisive people. If we let ourselves and our fellow-citizens be herded down such artificially imposed divergent roads, our country is in for an unfortunate, unnecessary, and destructive battle.

Let me share a list of reasons for not imposing our particular faiths into politics and the laws of our land. Before I get into the details, let me reassure those of you who identify yourselves as Evangelical Christians. Your faith has as much legitimacy as anybody's, and even your desire to share your faith isn't a problem. The problem arises when you try to impose your belief system on others.

Here's the list:

1. You wouldn't want others to impose their religious beliefs on you, so don't do it to them. (Remember, "Do unto others as…")
2. Respect for freedom of speech, religion, etc. is a fundamental ideal in the Constitution.
3. **Religion at the level of the individual's heart can solve problems, but religion at the level of public policy or law creates problems.** Just check what

the Taliban accomplished. (If you're tempted to say "Yeah, but they had the wrong religion," there are Christian examples.)

4. Having the humility to accept others' religious faiths as being just as legitimate as yours, and just as likely to be right, is a very constructive step toward peace. (Remember, humility is a Christian virtue.)

5. Recognizing that among the many reasons you are a Bible-believing Christian is the coincidence that you were born into it, and that religious beliefs themselves are things of the heart and therefore impossible to objectively verify can help you relax and not feel driven to convince or coerce others.

6. Remember Christ's attitude and approach? He set out to positively impact the quality of individual's lives by affecting their hearts and minds, not by trying to change the laws of the land.

Lest the Christians among us feel too picked-on, let me clearly state that to impose anti-religion is as wrong as imposing a particular religion. I don't live around many Jews or Muslims, but if I did I wouldn't have any trouble responding in a friendly and gracious way to "Happy Hanukkah" or "Happy Ramadan." To have trouble accepting a wish for a Merry Christmas is ridiculous, and a Christmas tree, even on government property, is hardly a religious endorsement. That blends invisibly into "culture," whereas a nativity scene may well be on that slippery slope we're better off avoiding. Who needs it on government property when we have all the freedom in the world to put it on our church or private property?

As we started out noting though, just as anti-religion can get carried to ridiculous extremes, the religious right can get carried away too. When the most important qualification for an appointed judge is that "_____ is a person of faith," when the new right knows best how to teach "science," when big government is the enemy until it is enforcing their values, then we know we've got some things badly out of whack. To those who might still insist on thumping your Bibles into others' lives, at least preface your comments with something like, "In my view of God…" And don't even try the "It's not my view, it's the Biblical view," approach. Firstly, pick the right text and even slavery and racism are Biblical. Secondly, it is arrogant to proclaim that the Bible is the only right view of God.

In a nutshell, if we can begin to relax and be less defensive about our beliefs, we can take our own faiths fairly seriously, but be accepting of others'. Despite our greatest worries, we're not going to fall apart as a nation because we're not following one particular view of "God's way;" however, we might fall apart because we quit respecting each other's values and religious freedom, including the conviction that there may be no god. For those who insist that America is a Christian Nation, imagine this: The Founding Fathers are faced with a choice. They can, A. form a government where faith (even our Christian faith) dictates the laws of the land, or B. establish a government which respects faiths of all kinds, and ensures that laws are based on our Constitution. You don't have to imagine it. They chose B. Some may not like the term "Secular," but that is exactly what our government was designed to be.

Critics of the secular nation ideas expressed here take multiple angles. One of these is to point to the demographics of our Founding Fathers in particular and of the early colonies in general, and to equate our obvious majority Christian "heritage" with "form of government." This mistaken equating of majority statistics with form of government isn't the end of trouble with semantics. Some have real trouble with the word "secular." They seem to feel secular means evil at worst, or devoid of any values at best. Without resorting to dictionary definitions, I would simply suggest that the laws of a secular nation are based on "common ground" between religious groups of all sorts and non-religious groups, and on "common sense." The "common ground" part necessarily involves not letting any single group, even a Christian majority, establish totalitarian or theocratic rule.

Another argument with the secular nation idea focuses on the fundamental idea of religious "truth." They insist that the Jesus of the Bible is the only way. They reject the idea that religious faiths of all kinds involve leaps of "faith," and they try to convince themselves and others that religious truth is based on evidence and that they have the objective truth. It is not my goal to disprove anyone's faith; indeed no faith can be disproved any more than it can be proved. Still, I will point to some realities that lend support to my assertion that faith needs to be held in humility to be constructive (items 4 and 5 on my list). One of those realities is that many within Christianity like selected facts found in archaeology from recent millennia, but never bother to really explore the deeper times, evidence, or issues of paleontology, molecular biology, astronomy, or the details of other faiths. That's okay. Most don't explore so comprehensively; but they shouldn't assume that the reality they've bothered to become aware of is anything near actual full-scale reality.

I do not mean to discount the deeply personal "evidence" that some feel they must consider. I simply think that they would do well to recognize that others have different personal evidence too, and that none of it is objectively verifiable.

In fighting against the secular nation idea, some resort

to quoting famous patriots or Supreme Court justices whose opinions were that we are a Christian nation. Patrick Henry is sometimes held up as an advocate of the Christian nation, but I for one can't believe he was so narrow-minded and shortsighted as to offer to die for only his particular flavor of liberty. As to the Supreme Court, it is ironic that the same people who decry it for failure and faulty logic in cases where they don't like the decision, quote it as an authority beyond question when it concluded that we are a Christian nation. The troublesome reality is that we as citizens have the responsibility of "reviewing" the opinions rendered by the court, and of recognizing when it speaks from its historical context more than from any objective truth. Remember, for almost three quarters of a century, even the Supreme Court let slavery stand.

Some express the concern that if we don't have God, the Ten Commandments, and the prospect of hell, our society will fall apart at the seams because nobody will have a reason to behave. Well, it makes one wonder why we have laws on the books, and punishments to go with them, intended to give structure and stability to our society. More to the point though, the people who feel that fear of punishment from God is the central stabilizing factor in society have pretty low levels of moral development. Without getting too lost in the details, many may vaguely remember from something like Psychology 101 that Lawrence Kohlberg did some interesting research which showed a progression of moral development.

Kohlberg's three broad levels were:

1. Pre-conventional. Here, as is typical in young children, decisions of right or wrong are made on punishment vs. reward, and on the perceived power of the rule-maker.

2. Conventional. Here decisions of right or wrong are made based on respect for the expectations of the family, group, or nation. It involves conforming to social conventions.

3. Post-conventional. Here decisions of right or wrong are made autonomously based on principles that have validity beyond group borders and without consideration of enforcement or consequence.

Interestingly, many people do not mature beyond level one. But that should not be used as an excuse to keep some particular religion and God central in society. There may be various reasons to keep a personal belief in God, but religion's role in controlling societal behavior becomes pretty shallow thinking. There are other effective motivations for good behavior. I want my kids to be able to say "Dad was a good, if far from perfect, man," and I want to feel that I will leave the world a better place than I found it.

In discussion with a few friends, some have pointed out that they suspect that the secularist's recognition that there may well be no God is a subconscious move of convenience. They explain that they see the 'doubter' as dismissing God so that he or she can get on with the feel-good experience of the moment. Any of us with a church-going background have probably heard a sermon on the shallowness and evil of the "if it feels good, do it" mentality. Well, for anyone to drop their hope that the universe has a stable *forever* in the hands of an eternal and loving God is hardly doing something because it feels good. On the contrary, the insistence that there is a loving and everlasting God who will ensure eternal life to His followers is the ultimate in doing (believing) something because it feels good. Facing like a grownup the uncomfortable possibility or probability that this life is it, that we have no supernatural solutions coming to rescue us from our shortsightedly self-made hell on earth is hardly "feel-good." A real adult can get past the sense of loss; we can focus on the real responsibilities and the hope of leaving a decent and enjoyable earth to future generations, and we can find joy in every step we accomplish towards that.

Some have said that I'm a dreamer to imagine that people, including the general masses, can get past the fixation on wishful thinking, on faith or religion, on believing what makes them feel secure and good, and instead focus on responsible choices for the best of humankind in general. As great a thinker as Carl Jung, in abandoning his original faith, said that "Only the wise are ethical from sheer intellectual presumption, the rest of us need the eternal truth of myth." My reply is that when the British nobles cornered King John into signing the Magna Carta, they did so to increase their own rights and limit the king's power. At that time, nearly eight centuries ago, they never would have imagined an eighteen-year-old non-property-owning black girl, or any other of us regular folk today, casting an informed and intelligent vote. They intentionally took a small step in the evolution of democracy, but inadvertently helped democracy take eventual steps far beyond what they would have thought was possible or wise – and look how far we've come! If we can grow, however slowly, into a reasonable depth and quality in democracy, we can surprise ourselves in other tough areas like overcoming the hope for supernatural solutions, and taking responsibility for our choices and actions, and genuinely looking out for the future good of humanity.

Some complain that secularists are trying to completely exclude Christian influence from government. Though I suspect there are extremist secularists out there (witness the whole Merry Christmas/Christmas tree spat) whose agenda may include complete exclusion, I think that most who assert that we are a secular nation are simply seeking to ensure that no faith be allowed to dominate our government as some in the neo-conservative movement seem to want. I think most any of us would have a hard time finding a better starting point for the laws of the land than "Treat others like you would like to be treated."

In wrapping up this section on the role of religion in our society, and therefore in our conflicts with other societies, I guess the simplest summary is to say "Let's keep some humility in our faiths, and let's not impose any of our faiths into government policy, domestic or foreign." Let's recognize that despite some of our fondest wishes, religion is extra-rational. Many people in many religions don't have too much trouble with that, but to the more fundamentalist Christians among us, I offer you this challenge: Set up a jury of peers from around the world, an educated person from every faith you can think of, including your precise brand of Christianity. Now let them try to convince one another with their objectively verifiable "facts." You know as well as I do how far they would, or rather wouldn't get.

Yes, the Founding Fathers went out of their way to ensure that our government would respect faiths of all kinds, yet establish none. If you are offended by the term secular, find another one to describe it. The bottom line is that religious freedom, and every other freedom, implies respect for and a degree of understanding and acceptance of our differences. None of that leads to imposed values. Don't resent it, celebrate it; it could be someone else imposing their values on you.

True die-hards will never be convinced, and I can live with that; it's the majority of my fellow middle-Americans who think issues through whom I hope I've given some food for thought. Why do I write, why do I risk the anger of some, why do I care? Because in this day and age, when we as a nation and culture are under attack from extremist terrorists, it is all too easy for us to succumb to our fears and lack of understanding and to lash out reflexively, thus widening a conflict that could be narrowed. Whether we like it or not, the world is increasingly a global village. We can fill the role of constructive leader, who not only seeks our own security, but the general good of all. Conversely, we can be as primitive and divisive as our current enemies in being dead sure that our particular belief system is exactly right and everyone should just fall in line. In case a borderline die-hard will consider a little gem of wisdom from a long-time conservative, I would suggest reading George F. Will's "Last Word" article in the May 23, 2005 *Newsweek*. His closing paragraph states, "America is currently awash in an unpleasant surplus of clanging, clashing, certitudes. That is why there is a rhetorical bitterness absurdly disproportionate to our real differences. It has been well said that the spirit of liberty is the spirit of not being too sure that you are right…."

A personal post-script to Christians

I genuinely hope that, after reading the whole, those who were irate after reading the previous rather direct simple truths have found room to relax. I'm not attacking Christians; nearly everyone near and dear to me is a Christian, and I wouldn't attack them. I'm not saying Christian beliefs are "wrong." Rather, I'm simply saying that since there is no way of objectively proving that they're "right," it is best, wisest, and most contributing to broad peace among man to hold our beliefs with humility. I know some who, for deep reasons of their own, can't stand the thought that their beliefs systems may not be "right," and I am sorry if I've shaken your sense of security.

A Word to Muslims

If you are a Muslim and have read the preceding pages, you are most probably a moderate and deserving of respect because you read broadly, risking exposure to ideas which may be different than yours. You think things through for yourself. Being a moderate who reads a variety of sources, you would know that I am not alone in America or the West in calling on our fellow moderates to step up and confront our radicals. You would know that we moderates recognize our national mistakes and are taking steps to correct them. We moderates, Christian *and* secular, can best limit our radicals here; we are on the inside. And you should know that you, Muslim moderates, can best limit the growth and affects of your radicals within Islam; you are on the inside.

This is no trivial side point. It is deadly serious. Unfortunately for you, your radicals advocate extremes of violence that I don't believe you can find in any branch of any other religion. Your challenge is indeed a big one, but you must step up to it. We outsiders to Islam can't get the attention of your radicals, we often don't know precisely who they are, and they won't listen to our logic anyway.

Your radicals won't be easily inclined to listen to your logic either, but you at least have a beginning point. You must recognize and outspokenly condemn the wrong aspects of radical Islam. It is not just the West that you would be helping in wrestling control away from your radicals; you will be helping yourselves, and all of humanity.

You have to know that if your radicals continue to gain influence, we in the West won't continue to act in as limited a fashion in our opposition to radical Islam's growth. If you don't step up, you will have proved that our radicals, who believe virtually all of Islam is violent, were right. And you will have given them the necessary excuse some of them are looking for to justify all-out broad cultural war. It is the hope of avoiding that exact scenario that drives me to write this book.

To make the challenge you face concrete and specific, let me mention a number of steps which I trust you will ultimately agree are reasonable. **You need to recognize that religious freedom is a good thing, and speak out and take action in its favor.** If you don't want Hindus or Christians forcing their religion on you, surely you can embrace the general idea that religious freedom is good for all. The practice of not even allowing your own people to choose their religion while actively exporting Islam with the sword (or bomb) simply does not recognize religious freedom, and you need to begin to change that.

You need to confront imams and others who advocate the spread of Islam by violent means. You need to proclaim with words and actions that Israel has a right to exist without constant threat. You need to oppose your radicals who seek to control all aspects of societal behavior by one set of religious laws. It is ridiculous that an Islamic community within a sovereign nation would demand to be able to impose Islamic law in any part of that country.

As a simple practical matter, you can't imagine that the West will passively watch as you let violence come out from among you or as you progressively exercise forced control over communities in our countries. You must know that we can't judge your attitudes, behavior, and motives based on how well you behave when you are a small minority. Rather, we must look to places where you are either a large minority or a majority. Based on that we can reasonably determine if it is in fact safe and wise to continue to grant you the same freedoms we grant to all other religions. If you reveal yourself to be a cancer which grows quietly until it takes over with a vengeance, you will find yourself being treated like a cancer. You can reveal yourself to not at all be a cancer.

Many of us in the West are taking risks to prevent the further broadening of our battle with terrorists into a battle between cultures. You too must step up and take risks to outnumber and "out-voice" your radicals in order to help avoid a battle that could devastate civilization. We, moderates in the West **and** moderates within Islam, must work *together* to narrow the conflict. We are working on our side, you must work on your side. You can continue to monitor our words and our actions (including our votes). Show us with your words and actions that we can count on you too. At this point many of us are still convinced that you do *want* to avoid a disastrous conflict. Let's share that goal, and actively work towards it! I know that some progress is being made on this front, but more is needed. If either of us fails, it will get very ugly and tragic for all of humanity.

It is worth remembering that our best chance at having some degree of logic prevail, at limiting the radical impulse for war, is when things are the least stressed. This puts urgency on our mission**. It is human nature that when things look scariest and most hopeless, more people resort to irrational beliefs, be they cultural or religious or both. If we keep creeping closer to all-out cultural war, it will get harder and harder to avoid.** *Now* is the time for clear thinkers to step up and help our respective cultures step back from the brink.

Post-script to Muslims

If by any chance you have read only these few pages addressed to you, you will have the mistaken impression that I am promoting nothing but typical anti-Islamic propaganda. If you now go back and read the last two chapters in their entirety you will discover quite the opposite. Please read the whole before you reach any conclusions.

Chapter 5.

Confidence vs. Cockiness:
Reflections on Leadership

In looking at the world in which we find ourselves with a focus on how we can affect the battle against terrorism, we would do well to think seriously about how cultural or national leaders affect the fights the people find themselves in. What characteristics or tendencies of leaders may help maximize the chances of a stable and peaceful world, and what characteristics do the opposite? Do personal belief systems make leaders any more or less prone to put us all at risk of war? How would any particular leader identify the most important thing anyone needs to know about him, and what does that itself say about him? What are we willing to follow? Where and how far are we willing to go?

Of course we all have a tendency to follow leaders who articulate positions we personally subscribe to, but let's attempt to suspend personal attachment for a moment in objectively analyzing where those positions, applied to public and foreign policy, might take us. Obviously people tend to vote for and follow leaders whom they think, at least for the moment, are correct in the positions they advocate, the beliefs they hold. But a good question to ask ourselves might be "What if our leaders turn out to be wrong in some of their basic assumptions and positions? Are there intrinsic risks to certain positions?"

Let's apply this to some positions on a few of the sides surrounding our battle with terrorism. On one side we have fundamentalist Muslim leadership, represented by Osama bin Laden and perhaps some radical mullahs. The most important thing they would want you to know about them is that they are true believers in Islam. They believe they are called to take over the world for Allah. If you were a regular Muslim citizen of some country and you were evaluating whether or not these are leaders worth following, you would benefit from going through the following thought sequence: If he happens to be right, spreading Islam by the sword will work out okay in the end. Yes infidels will suffer, but that's okay you say because you think they should suffer. And if you and yours suffer and die in the cause of right, that will work out okay in the long run too.

The thought sequence continues. What if they are not right? Is death and destruction on all sides something that should at least trouble you? The world as a whole, all of humanity including your own people, will have suffered because you chose to follow leaders who didn't look at the big picture, who were so sure of their rightness that they went for destruction over the basic values of human rights.

Let's look for a moment now at some of our fundamentalist Christian leaders. They too are sure of what they believe, and many would say that the most important thing about them is their faith in God. They see Jesus Christ coming back to save true believers from an earthly mess. Some of them tend not to worry one iota about the environment because "We're only going to be here for a little while longer." Many of them believe in a world-ending Apocalypse. Again, the same thought sequence ought to be instructive.

If they're right, everything will work out okay for Christian believers.

But what if they're wrong? All of humanity will inherit a worse environment, and if we willingly walk into an apocalyptic scenario, imagine how many will die needlessly because we, like our current enemies, let religious conviction enter into and direct how we conduct foreign policy.

Some might leap to the conclusion that I am advocating electing only atheist leaders. No; that's too simplistic. I simply think we should ask, "How high up the list of self-description does a leader's religious faith sit?" If it is at or very near the top, following that person means we are embracing risks that go along with seeing life through one unique tint of shaded glasses – ones that could turn out to be wrong.

We can continue to elect people of faith. Many have a religiously based belief system, but a tempered one. A belief system that recognizes faith as faith, and that it includes a 'leap.' This type of person recognizes the equal validity of other faiths, and is careful to keep the perspective of their faith separate from judgements of best pragmatic and principled policy.

Let's apply the same test to the leader whose faith ranks much lower on the scale of self-description, who holds his faith with more humility and with less absolute certainty. If this type of leader applies his broad and relatively secular view, we and all of humanity stand our best chance for quality survival because unnecessary religiously driven wars are avoided. And what if they were wrong in making decisions based on their best assessment of the long-term good of our country and humanity as a whole without any particular religious perspective? Well, whichever "God" turns out to be right will still salvage and save what He wanted to anyway, so no unnecessary harm will have been done, to anyone.

It may be worth noting that our historic tendency to trust politicians of faith is a bit of a funny thing. Have we learned anything from the priest-pedophile tragedies? It should be obvious that the outward manifestations of religiosity, be they clothing or talk, are no guarantee of good character. Indeed, there are recent examples from within politics where avowed Christians were taking bribes, intimidating colleagues, and otherwise behaving in obviously un-Christ-like ways.

One hopes that in an educated and reflective society we would begin to realize that:

 # 8. The faith of a politician should be a side issue, as long as it isn't among his top self-descriptors; at that point it becomes a risk.

The tendency to strongly and narrowly *believe* in one's faith has often been mistaken for personal confidence, a characteristic we like in leaders. Notice though that the confidence that makes one closed to new information and alternate points of view is actually much shallower than the personal confidence that makes one able to be open to new information and points of view. In truth:

 # 9. Real confidence is based in knowing *how* best to think things through, to continue to figure things out and wisely adjust to realities in life, not simply in knowing *what* you believe now and forever.

I find myself hoping that we will develop the habit of electing presidents who will choose to include in their innermost circle of advisors a person with whom they very often disagree, but whom they deeply respect. A president with the confidence to expose his ideas to strong and informed criticism, and to listen carefully to and think deeply on other points of view would be much less prone to enormous errors that have lasting consequences and may take generations to reverse. It is up to us to reject leaders with shallow confidence and false bravado, and to elect leaders with sufficiently deep confidence to be able to remain open to perspectives they didn't happen to grow up with and may not initially like. We, voters, must begin to tell the difference between the two types of confidence.

I am at times hopeful that we are beginning to learn. Let's hope that the leaders we choose will avoid being ideologues, and that they will not only be open to learning, but will cultivate the tendency to seek an understanding of new angles and of gathering new and sometimes surprising information. (It is interesting to note that a leader who is truly open to new ways of looking at things will probably be accused, by a group which emphasizes sticking with traditional understanding, of being an ideologue of the liberal stripe. Hopefully that accusation is transparent to most.)

To reiterate a point made near the end of chapter 3, if we find ourselves as a nation in circumstances we really don't like, let's resist the temptation to point fingers at the leaders who put us in those circumstances. I fairly quickly came to mistrust and dislike Bush, Cheney, Rumsfeld, and Rove, much like many others across our fair land. But getting my blood pressure up over their unbelievably poor decisions was kind of useless. Although many of us found ourselves profoundly depressed the day after the 2004 election, we couldn't really blame our leaders. "We," too many of the people, had put these misguided ideologues back in power, and it was, and still is, up to all of us to learn from experience.

The warnings had been more than adequate. Bush had already revealed that he was closed to new and real information. His statement that, "I know what I believe and I believe what I believe." should have been easy to translate in all of our heads; his conclusions were set, and nothing was going to change his mind. From Iraq to failure on the environment, from being part of the corporate greed wave to losing old allies while gaining new enemies, the combination of arrogance and ignorance was plenty clear at least well before the 2004 election.

I must comment here on the wisdom of our Founding Fathers in creating a republic with three branches of government, each vested with powers that would check the powers of the others. It seems as though we have grown progressively to focus the term 'leadership' almost exclusively on the executive branch. Indeed it seems as if the legislative branch itself has gone almost as a lamb to the slaughter in submitting to executive signing statements and the like. I can only hope that near future congresses will choose to grow a spine and recognize the simple wisdom I found on a colleague's classroom wall – "Leaders: those with good judgment who are not afraid, when necessary, to point out the poor judgment of others." Congressmen and women with the insight and ability to articulate where and when executive judgment is poor are sorely needed, and the same can be said of citizens.

Indeed, rather than pointing fingers at leaders, we need to look in the mirror. We must get better at choosing leaders who articulate in clear terms their commitment to process (thinking), not just endpoint (belief). We must get better at recognizing and choosing deep confidence, the kind that can say "Now wait a minute, I hadn't thought of it that way before. Where did you get that information; is it verifiable?" And we must get better at recognizing false bravado, the kind that is smug, cocky, and knows it all already. That shallow confidence will lead all right – straight to trouble we won't like.

If we cultivate the ability to see through the superficial it will help us realize that *claims* of honest effort on the part of a leader don't make it *so*. In his last weeks in office President Bush (W) conceded that "...people have disagreed with my decisions, but they've been made with a lot of deliberation, and they've been made with one thing in mind: what's best for the United States of America." (NPR interview; 1-5-09) Wow. The lack of honest introspection ought to strike us all forcefully. More than being made based on "deliberation," his administration clearly tended to make decisions based on ideology. This involved preset conclusions, often apparently based on his religious views of life and conflict. Responsibility for the quality of decisions made by our leaders does come back to us, to how thoroughly we think things through, and how carefully we vote.

Chapter 6.

Theater of the Absurd:
Endless Excuses for Having Invaded
Iraq, and Lessons to be Learned

Although we can all hope that our involvement in Iraq is slowly and genuinely winding down, just putting it behind us and forgetting about it would be a serious mistake. There are important lessons that many of us seem to want to ignore. If we care to learn from history, however recent, and avoid repeating unnecessary mistakes, we can't ignore the lessons of Iraq.

In Chapter 4 on the role of religion in our current conflict with terrorists, when dealing with the simple truth that we are a secular nation we looked specifically at common arguments that have been used against the secular idea. Though I don't want to get sidetracked into an everyday blog of arguments about what our involvement in Iraq has done to our battle against terrorism, the fact that there are quite a few common arguments attempting to justify our being there which are so seriously flawed they approach the absurd motivates me to look specifically at them too. Further, so much attention has been paid to discussing the relative merits or glaring errors of various specific strategic decisions that we often overlook learning the biggest and most important lessons. Really learning though, means we must re-evaluate what are too often set beliefs. Although Iraq has faded from the everyday public consciousness, we must seriously look at some of our beliefs about our involvement there in order to actually learn. Let's try.

Some have said that one of the reasons we weren't able to secure a fairly quick win in Iraq is because we weren't ruthless enough. They've said that nice guys finish last, and that pacifists die at the hands of the aggressive. You would think from this argument that we won World War II by being more ruthless than the Japanese or Germans. We can be proud of the fact that we weren't. Indeed, sometimes truth and right can prevail with the necessary toughness and perseverance, but without ruthlessness.

Some quickly argue that we were ruthless in bombing the heck out of the Germans and A-bombing the Japanese, civilians included. We did the necessary degree of ruthlessness, but our behavior on the whole was civilized. That I know of, we forced no death marches and had no extermination camps. More to the point though, the enemies we battled were whole, united populations, nations. We had to fight them all because they were all out to get us.

It is very different now. There are extremist segments who are out to get us, but they do not represent whole nations or cultures. We must fight those extremists, not only physically but mentally. We must be smart enough to not draw in the whole culture that surrounds the extremists. If you are one who accepts the idea that the whole Muslim culture must be fought, you are buying into an impossible fight. History demonstrates that you cannot eliminate a religion. A major factor in the growth of the early Christian church was persecution. The more you persecute any people of faith, the more their faith will grow, it's just that way. We don't have to be on the dumb end of that lesson again. With wisdom, toughness, selectiveness, and perseverance we can fight terrorism without unnecessarily and mistakenly drawing in a whole culture.

An incredible irony of the argument in favor of a more ruthless approach is that out of the self-same mouths have come acknowledgements that this is a battle of ideas, that this is a potential turning point in history. It *is* a battle of ideas. As often expressed, it is a battle for hearts and minds, and it has every possibility of being a turning point in history – that is the driving force for my dealing with this topic. The question that I trust we recognize crying out for an answer is: Can we honestly hope to win a battle of ideas by being the most ruthless?!

The ruthless idea brings to mind the media battles over alleged and apparent war atrocities committed by a few of our forces. I trust we civilians keep in mind that most of us don't have a clue what it's like to be in a firefight where a moment's hesitation could cost you your life. I also trust that our forces keep foremost in their minds that we must maintain (or try to regain) the moral high ground. We can make lasting enemies in a moment's indiscretion, and it can take generations to build trusting friendships. Unfortunately we have given our troops an almost impossibly tall order in trying to "maintain" the higher moral ground because we are where we shouldn't be to begin with.

Another convoluted argument begins with the idea that in the fight with terrorism we need a "front" that is somewhere specific, and we don't want it here. So far, so good. Some connect to this the idea that Saddam Hussein was a Hitler wanna-be, that our battle in Iraq is like WWII, and that if we didn't take him on he would have marched progressively outward. To this some add the notion that our being in Iraq is like us helping defend Great Britain against Hitler. Some push it still further in saying that we can use Iraq as a critical beachhead nation from which we can launch a counter-offensive in attempting to retake territory under the bad-guy's control.

We will have to come back to the above paragraph in several parts. First, yes, Saddam was a Hitler wanna-be, he was one bad dude. But his expansionist ideas were dealt an appropriate blow in the Gulf War of 1990, lead by the senior George Bush and a broad coalition. Oh, Saddam still had bad wishful dreams, but under the watchful eye of the international community and effective no-fly zones, that's essentially all they were. Can we really run around imposing our will because we think (and have good reason to) that some leader is a bad guy? **Does force-feeding our version of democracy, whether the prerequisites to stable democracy are in place or not, make it an appealing and effective diet – or a despised foreign thing?**

Second, the battle in Iraq can't be remotely compared to WWII for numerous reasons. In WWII we had long-time allies begging and pleading for us to get out of our isolationist mode and get involved. Before Iraq we had allies initially urging caution and then flat out distancing themselves from us. Before America's formal involvement in WWII we had German U-boats sinking scattered ships in our merchant marine fleet and then Japan attacking Pearl Harbor; WWII was clearly *not* a war of choice, Iraq even more clearly *was*. Further, virtually everyone in Britain wanted us there helping them avoid being conquered by an aggressive foreign invader; the contrasts with Iraq shouldn't need more enumerating.

The most enormous error though is skirted around so often that many seem to forget it. Notice that the arguments three paragraphs back entangle the war on terror with the war in Iraq. We already had a specific front in the war on terror – Afghanistan. Saddam was not in bed with al-Qaida; that didn't make him trustworthy, but it did and still does mean we didn't have the same universally accepted justification for invading Iraq as we did Afghanistan.

An irony of the WWII comparisons involves remembering how grateful all the Allied nations can be that Hitler lost focus on the Battle of Britain and opened up the front with the Soviet Union. That dilution and dispersal of German forces was incalculably costly to them. **No doubt al-Qaida is equally grateful for our opening up the front in Iraq.** The biggest reason for their gratitude though goes far beyond diluting our forces. **The difference it made and will make for some time to come in their recruiting ability is where the real pay-off for them lies.** As pointed out in Chapter 3, many Muslims/Arabs who might have stayed as relative moderates, when faced with a bullying giant who was forcing his way where he didn't have just cause, began to drift into the arms of extremists. We can only thank the lack of reasonable insight and foresight on the part of too many of our own ideologues.

So can Iraq, under our control or influence, serve as a launch point for our war on terror? In reality:

 # 10. If our presence is perceived as unjustified by the Muslim world, as is the case with Iraq but wasn't with Afghanistan, we are probably serving to recruit more future terrorists than we are killing today. Is that a winning formula?

We desperately need to achieve some reasonable level of stability in Iraq, and then get the heck out! Some don't like various apologies for past mistaken judgment coming from the Obama administration, but those exact national *mea culpas* may well do something toward reducing a major al-Qaida recruiting tool. It is not a bad thing to admit when we were wrong! Here's hoping.

Sadly, not only has our unjustifiable invasion of Iraq set back our entire war on terror, it has also set back our efforts in Afghanistan to a degree which too many actually try to ignore. The resurgence of the Taliban there is broadly acknowledged to be directly related to both our diluted manpower there and to an upturn in the level of motivation among extremists. Yes, *our* actions can motivate and recruit for our enemies. This is sadly crystal clear.

We are going to struggle to simply stop the downward spiral and begin to make positive progress in Afghanistan, and then to possibly bring that country to a reasonable position of stability and development. The decisions and lessons along the way will be tough. While we debate the merits or faults of various approaches we may take there, let us never lose sight of how we complicated our own lives by taking our eye off the ball when we first let ourselves be led off to a fight of our choosing in Iraq.

In summarizing these extremely brief comments on Afghanistan, allow me this plea: To my fellow-Americans who are not hawks from the right, please, dig up your best patience and perseverance, but also keep thinking and ana-lyzing evidence. I still think that we must stick things out in Afghanistan. Even the perception there that we might start to waiver is very damaging. We had just cause in going there and, as long as we're not staying for some material/imperial gain, we must see things through. Those people are not fools. They'll know if our motives are right and if we have the courage and stick-to-itiveness to hang in there through the rough times. The ultimate price we and the broader world may pay if we don't help bring Afghanistan to stability through development will be a price we won't want to pay. That being said, in late 2009 Matthew Hoh, a Marine with Afghanistan battlefield experience who later went back there working for the State Department, gave us all some serious food for thought on the realities of the situation there, and what we can hope to achieve. (I encourage you to Google and read his letter of resignation.) Our presence there in 2010 and beyond may well have little in common with why we initially went there clear back in 2001.

A major part of the bottom line is simply that:

11. We can't run around deposing dictators we don't like. In imposing our will around the world, what would that make us?

This doesn't mean we have to sit idly by while various forms of Kosovo, Rwanda, or Darfur are repeated in unnumbered places. For one, where there are clear, massive, humanitarian crises created by bad regimes, it will be broadly recognized by the vast majority of nations, and we could form a coalition of more than a handful. Most importantly, we wouldn't be viewed as bullying and serving our own interests, as long as we didn't stay and dictate nation-building our way for our gain. Secondly, **we can in fact be involved in spreading democracy, not by force, but by working with people to create the prerequisite conditions.**

We could make a great difference in local attitudes in mineral-rich countries which almost don't have a middle class. The Jihadists would not find such easy footholds. This would *not* mean eliminating existing governments, but rather working with them to develop their educational systems and broaden the economic base of activity.

I can't possibly address all the hawkish arguments in favor of our fight in Iraq. The fact is that ideologues will no doubt keep coming up with new variations on the theme while trying to justify it. My hope is simply that more and more of us will begin to thoughtfully analyze the underpinnings of our recent foreign policy, and assert our voices, demanding decisions based on logic, evidence, and breadth of vision, not just beliefs. To repeat the lesson we must not forget when next we contemplate a fight: **there is no right way to fight the wrong war.**

Preface to
Section III:
America's Durable
Internal Stability

From this point on, the simple truths I present have nothing to do with the immediate urgency of dealing with a world affected by terrorism. Rather they have to do with attempting to look down the long road for our nation and culture, and for humanity as a whole. In about fifteen years America will hit the 250 year mark. These years will bring plenty of challenges. Assuming we navigate those successfully, we need to begin thinking more and more of what will be good for our great-grandchildren, and their great-grandchildren. In fact, part of what may well help us get through the next couple of decades intact could be that we begin *now* to think and act with the long run in mind. What we want now, politically and otherwise, can't continue to be the driving force behind our decisions. If we get better at thinking of what we want for our great-grandchildren we might realistically imagine that our descendents may one day be approaching the celebration of 500 years for our democracy.

Interestingly, while we view the world in a competitive way as we must, it is likely true that what is really good for America in the long run will also be good for the rest of the world, and vice-versa. Thus we need to not only think of the best good of our children's children, but also of humanity as a whole. No, we don't want one world government, but we do want a stable world. If we think and act only for the immediate and only for ourselves, the world at large is likely to become a decidedly less stable place. (I must take this opportunity to make one more book recommendation. Jeffrey Sacks' *The End of Poverty* makes the case, both so broadly and with such detail and depth, for constructive involvement in raising the quality of life for all. If you're a doubter, this is a must-read.)

To bring us back home in our focus though, let's for the moment remember that part of winning against terrorism means we must avoid a power vacuum in the world at large, which means that America's strength (and wisdom in using it) is needed. Further, broad economic and social stability at home is part of what is needed in order to maintain America's strength.

Economic and social stability involve many things. I suggest that our educational system is obviously a key component. Further, science education in particular is important both because of its role in maintaining our technological capabilities and because it so happens that science education is where part of the battle over religion's place in our nation is being waged. The key difference between objectively analyzing evidence and actually thinking things through vs. reasserting cherished beliefs is critical, and has an effect not only directly in scientific endeavors but also in applied social and political policy. This theme must continue in these domestic areas too.

A third very important area in maintaining economic and social stability at home involves fiscal policy (our approach to taxing ourselves and spending on ourselves). A balanced budget, based on a thorough review of realistic expectations and with a view to the good of our whole society, is desperately needed.

I cannot possibly deal with every significant issue which influences our economic and social stability at home. That fact is reflected in the chapter title "Too Many Topics – Not

Enough Time." Still, in this chapter I have chosen to deal with a few topics of vital and broad home-culture significance. These include: immigration, how soft and spoiled we are becoming, energy, and affirmative action and race relations.

In the midst of this I will pause to briefly point out the obvious: no amount of economic or social stability will count for anything if we don't manage to maintain ecological stability on a global level.

Again, join the discussion.

Chapter 7.

Nobody Left Behind –
But Who Gets Short-changed?:
Education in America Today

Working for nearly a decade in a private Christian educational system and now for over a decade in public education has given me more than my share of exposure to discussions of what's wrong and what's right in American education. Some of the most interesting observations and comments have come though, from outside the system. One remark I've heard more than once goes something like, "We'll fund education to a better degree when they improve performance and put out a better product."

When I've asked whether the speaker expects to get improved performance by shifting class sizes from 22 to 32, particularly at the elementary level, they've looked a little surprised and uncomfortable. The topic then inevitably shifts to administrative waste and such. I, like any sane person, readily acknowledge the need for greater efficiency and the cutting of duplicated administrative (federal, state, local) costs. This immediate discussion serves to bring into focus two particularly important aspects of education: student performance and funding.

The ability to compare, based on first-hand experience, private and public education has been informative to me.

My students in parochial schools were no smarter on average, but I do have a much higher rate of sustained failure in public schools. Why? When I sent home an "F" to parents who were paying hard cash for their child's education, something happened. Failure didn't continue. In public schools I have sent home "F"s for six consecutive grading periods, and sadly in most cases nothing ever changed. The difference had to do with what parents would put up with, what expectations they set, and how they supported and reinforced their child's efforts.

This perfectly matches what I concluded at the end of my first year in public education, a year in which I was a substitute teacher. Having been reared in parochial schools, my extended family had many long-held reservations about public schools. When, at the end of that year of subbing, one family member asked me about the evils we had all feared in public schools I was able to reply, "There are lost kids going nowhere, dropping out. There are also kids who have their act completely together. Some going on scholarships to top-flight universities, some are doing great things in their home communities. And you know what? They've all gone through the same classrooms and schools. They've all had the same teachers. So what has made the difference? The home; what was expected, and what was supported."

This brings me to my first simple truth in education.

#12. It not only takes effort on the part of teachers and schools, it takes effort and support beyond the school to ensure that kids get good educations and that their performances improve.

Yes, the leverage I have as a teacher on a low performing student is limited. I can be thorough, I can set a high standard, and I can be creative. Shoot, I can stand on my head and do the hula. But I can't match the leverage that somebody at home, setting some basic expectations, can exert.

The irony here is that public schools have been made the whipping boys for poor performance, and most of this has come from the end of the political spectrum that often preaches personal accountability. The truth is that this is a broader societal issue. What can be done to hold children and parents accountable for their efforts and performance?

We don't need and don't want more big government, but we might benefit from broadening the discussion. Should various social benefits continue to go to the homes of under-performing students? Could after-school programs be required in some circumstances? Where would the funding for supplemental programs come from?

13. As with life in general, in education you tend to get what you pay for.

The far right has some competing and contradictory agendas about education. The emphasis on cutting taxes without regard to consequences has led to a decade of declining funding in education. One of the immediate consequences has been progressively larger class sizes. There is research that shows the importance of lower class size to student performance, but who really needs it? Surely it meets the common sense test to recognize that more can be accomplished with each individual student in a room full of 22 third graders than can be accomplished in a room full of 32 third graders. It is shortsighted and unrealistic to force larger class sizes while demanding improved performance!

One of the longer-term consequences of under-funding education may not come home to roost for a while yet, but I deem it worth mentioning now. While the echo of the echo of the Baby Boom begins coming through our schools, the number of teachers is on the decline. What about recruiting more? Well, from time to time teachers have students ask them, "What do you feel about a career in education? Are you glad you became a teacher?" And most of us (I trust) can honestly answer, "Yes." But when the questions go on and get more detailed, we have to concede things like, "Yes, you can make more in almost any other field with equivalent years of training and preparation." The trouble is that the sharp students, who are aware of the world, and perhaps a touch more materially minded than before, know that it is "substantially" more in a wide array of fields.

Does the future of education bode well if we become progressively less able to attract at least some of the best and the brightest? Raising the quality of teachers means raising standards of acceptance in college education programs. We also need to limit the number of times a candidate can try to pass the various tests of basic knowledge and skills to become a teacher. Yet those steps would further limit the number of teachers coming out. A major part of the solution to that, to making becoming a teacher a more competitive process while still turning out more teachers, is to make the profession more attractive to more talented young people. Are we doing that with perpetual under-funding?

14. Various aspects of "No Child Left Behind" and other federal mandates, including some involving "Highly Qualified" teachers, are unattainable or impractical goals.

Schools take in kids with the **full** range of abilities and backgrounds. To say that 100% of those kids, special ed, brand new English language learners, and others are going to pass various standardized tests is simply setting frustratingly unachievable goals for the students, parents, and teachers. If that 100% success mark were reached by even the slowest learners and the least prepared, wouldn't it simply be an indication that the bar was set so low that it would be a meaningless measure of "success" for the bulk of students? It's rather like wishing that everybody in the country were in sufficient cardiovascular health to be able to cover a mile in less than eight minutes, but since they aren't and can't, let's lower the standard to fifteen minutes.

Further, smaller rural schools will be able to offer fewer and fewer electives when teachers cannot teach a subject or two beyond their official endorsement areas. Who is being served when, for political reasons, laws are made that limit what electives are available to students in small-school rural America?

15. The huge emphasis on pulling up the performance of our low and marginal students is taking time and effort away from talented and/or motivated students.

If the parents of talented or motivated students, or for that matter average students, could sit in class and see the level of effort and time spent on clarification, re-explanation, and re-illustration that goes on in the name of pulling up the lowest performing students in an effort to help them meet the minimum standards, they would be appalled. I used to feel confident that we were able to prepare the talented or motivated kids to compete in university programs with privileged kids from elite private schools. Now our talented or motivated are to an even greater degree "on their own" when it comes to getting the most out of their high school education. If this trend continues, the gap between their prep experience and that of the privileged elite could become so large that I don't know if any but the extreme exception will be able to compete.

Consider one more specific case of well-intended educational policy shift which actually has negative consequences. Various levels of educational policy-makers have decided that the minimum credits required for high school graduation should be increased in key areas like science and math. Sounds good, right? Well, stop and look carefully at the end result. In a subject that was, up until now, an *elective* like Algebra II or Chemistry, we had university-aiming students who were ready and willing to really focus. For the first time they were free of their less-than-focused peers and the whole elective class was therefore able to step on the gas and make a lot of forward progress.

With the new requirements of a third year of math and science, the whole gamut of students will be stepping into classes that had previously been electives. For many of these students, university preparation is the last thing on their list of interests, and for some of them it is really beyond their grasp. I know, that's politically incorrect, but denying the realities of the bell curve doesn't make it go away. The bell curve is an undeniable truth whether one is measuring height, foot size, or intelligence. Don't lose sight of the important point here: because of this shift to a higher *minimum* standard for all students, **less** will actually be accomplished for the ready and willing students. Those previously elective classes will inevitably be dumbed-down. Those who we should be doing a thorough job of preparing for the university of their choice will actually be even less prepared than before. This particular problem can be reasonably solved in large schools where specially created third year classes like "Chemistry in the Community" or "Consumer Math" can fit into the schedule right alongside the university-track courses of real Chemistry and Algebra II, and others; the problem is insurmountable though in unnumbered smaller rural schools where you can't offer both the simplified and the real version of the course. Again, who is being served by such well-intended but poorly thought through policies? It is certainly not the students.

This is perhaps the **most important point** to be made on the current trend in education and our ability to stay strong and stable as a culture and nation. **We can't let a superficially commendable focus on the lowest groups keep public education from doing a thorough and quality job on the talented and motivated.** The end result of the current emphasis will be a permanent elite who, generation after generation, get their university preparation in private schools. Not everything or every group can be *the* top priority. Balanced emphasis would accept the reality that some may choose failure, and let us return some resources and effort where it may make the biggest difference.

 # 16. Anybody and everybody, however poorly educated their home background, can see the simple reality that putting effort into doing well in school opens up doors of opportunity in their future. They also know that lack of attention and resulting failure in school is going to result in closed doors and dead-end jobs.

The point here is not the fact that doors of opportunity are opened or shut based on one's level of achievement in school, rather, it is that **everybody does know this fact.** There is choice involved. Remember the good old expression "You can lead a horse to water, but you can't make it drink!" Think about this truth in the context of much of the political talk relative to education. Again, it is ironic that the group that generally puts the most vocal emphasis on personal accountability has led the charge in blaming "failing" schools.

Teachers can be expected to be well prepared, to be thorough, to be creative, to be fair, to work at motivating, to never give up on anyone or any group, to be professional, to set high standards, and to lead by example, but they can't be expected to **make** anyone (or everyone) learn. People can and unfortunately do choose to remain undereducated and ignorant. Interestingly, one can even argue that there is a place in the economy for unskilled labor, and that it really doesn't have to be all illegally imported, but that is its own topic for another chapter.

Having touched a number of times on reasonable expectations of teachers, I must acknowledge here that teachers' unions are learning that defending incompetence is a waste of resources. The business though of evaluating the job teachers do is not easy. One administrator might be insightful, helpful, and still demanding, while another is a know-it-all who has risen to his or her level of incompetence, and evaluates based on personal bias at best or straight up spite at worst. This is a difficult area, and continues to need both research and common sense, and much more than a cookie-cutter approach.

Now back to the unfortunate choices that some students make. I'm not arguing that everyone has the maturity to make wise choices when they are sixteen, let alone ten. I'm simply pointing out that no matter how lamentable their choice, and no matter how hard teachers work to help students eventually make different choices, in the end teachers and schools can't actually force wise choices on their students.

Some efforts aimed at improving our level of success with low performing groups, children of poverty for example, seem to focus on every imaginable angle of finding or imposing solutions from the 'outside.' I have witnessed next to nothing which has involved plainly explaining to young people that there will be clear expectations of their involvement, their choice of deliberate focused effort. One of our central battles with backgrounds of poverty is to begin to shift the individual's perceived locus of control. We need to help people stop seeing themselves as corks floating down a river – a situation where fate, the powerful, and all things beyond their reach determine their direction and destiny (what we call an external locus of control). Rather, we need to help people see themselves as having a motor and steering wheel – a condition of having a great degree of personal affect on the direction and outcome of their own lives (what we call an internal locus of control).

I believe that even relatively young people are actually pretty smart. If educational leaders articulate this important message in understandable ways, students and parents will not only 'get' the idea, they will embrace it. But it will take educational leaders with the courage to stop the excuse-making on behalf of the disadvantaged. Leaders of courage won't be afraid to accept that you really can't please all the people all the time. They will be less inclined toward political correctness, and more willing to step on toes (hopefully gently and constructively) when necessary. One specific aspect of this involves getting young people to accept that they don't have a right to disrespect their classmates' right to a quality learning environment with repeated interruptions. While we have zero tolerance for weapons and drugs, we seem to have infinite tolerance for habitual disruption, for disrespecting others' right to learn. It seems this official tolerance is based in a background of excuse-making. Are we doing young people any favors when we allow them to continue chaotic habits? Never mind being prepared for university, will these habits lead to success in the workplace?

Having mentioned children of poverty and the challenges of shifting their view of themselves in the world, it is interesting to note a few things. One, poverty in the American context hardly equals poverty in the global context. Secondly, in many cases here in America, and in most cases in developing countries, some families and students already actively embrace the idea that education is an opportunity, it is their ticket up and out. The trick seems to be how to get that idea to go viral. I believe a little more straight talk, a little clarification of personal rights vs. the rights of others would be a good first step.

If you are inclined to question my assertion here, check into an organization known as KIPP (Knowledge is Power Program). They have excelled – while specifically targeting underprivileged groups. But note part of how they start: they have teachers, parents, and students sign a Commitment to Excellence, and they have a short but powerful motto – "Work Hard. Be Nice." I can tell you that I've been witness to the slow but steady erosion of the proportion of students who buy into *hard work*.

A final note here to parents who already definitely get this, and who want their kids to be able to take full advantage of the opportunity that education is: many administrators in education tend to be a bit like typical politicians – they're quickest to grease the squeaky wheel. Parents, if you sit quiet while administrators' time and attention is taken up by various trouble spots, you and your wishes for an improved minimum quality of learning environment will be overlooked. If on the other hand you join together with other concerned parents of willing and motivated kids, including others from poor families, your cumulative squeak will be heard and will get some grease. (If you want to be able to share your concerns and your expectations with administrators from a highly informed perspective, a good book to read would be Richard Arum's *Judging School Discipline: The Crisis of Moral Authority.*)

To reiterate a point I made near the start of this chapter: educational problems are part of broader societal issues. The bottom line is that we need an educational philosophy and governmental expectations which acknowledge the role of personal choice, and a system which doesn't insist that all students follow the university prep track. No matter how enormous a role information and technology eventually play in our economy, we will still have a somewhat diverse job base and the need for differing levels of skill. And I'm not sure how much the shift away from Bush-era institutional punishment for failure and toward Obama's competition for resources helps us refocus on these basic realities.

It seems to me that it is becoming increasingly clear that we could learn something from educational systems which provide a two or three track system where some of the students are on the university prep track, and others are in various types of trade or vocational training. Note here that some form of 'tracking' wouldn't have to be imposed on students by any educational powers that be; in most cases student choice in selecting their classes, and therefore their track, would take care of which type of diploma they receive. Yes, if we learn to think things through, to look at the experience and results we and others get, to do more than believe what we set out believing, then we can learn from others and improve our educational policies and processes, and thus improve our product (our young people, and eventually, our society).

Chapter 8.

Intelligent Design vs. Evolution: Letting the Evidence Speak for Itself in Science Education

Continuing in education, but shifting gears...

The public debate over how best to teach science, specifically how to deal with evolution and whether intelligent design should be part of science or not, is obviously a very hot button. Again, I cover this topic with a degree of reluctance because some feel so intensely about it, but I discuss this issue anyway in the hope of helping us make decisions based on clear thinking and not on hot emotion. Let's try to work our way past blindly believing what we happened to inherit or like.

My career in education, both in private and in public schools, has been spent primarily in the field of science. I taught biology in Christian schools, and although I recently switched to social studies, I taught biology for over a decade in public school. I could deal with this in a dry way, but that only glosses over the depth of feelings involved; so, I am choosing to deal with it by sharing some of what I've experienced and learned along the way.

Before I became a teacher I obviously was a student, and I came up through Christian schools. What I learned about evolution and the fossil record was basically that any "pattern" or "sequence" was the result of selective perception or outright invention on the part of dishonest or deceptive atheist scientists. Among the criticisms directed at these evolutionists was that they formed their conclusions ahead of time and simply went about selecting evidence and creating theoretical explanations to support their prior conclusions. Once out of high school and into a Christian college in the mid 1970s, I learned that over the previous several decades conservative Christian scientists had moved away from denying the pattern and sequence in the fossil record. Rather, they had begun attempting to explain the sequence that was increasingly clear and undeniable.

I began to be exposed to literature put out by the Geoscience Research Institute (GRI), a conservative Christian organization founded in 1958 to find scientific support for traditional Biblical views of earth's history. I continued to read publications from this and other conservative sources, and while working as a biology teacher at a Christian high school in the mid 1980s had the privilege of being part of a weekend seminar lead by Dr. Robert Brown, then chairman of GRI. One question that was put to him sticks out clearly in my memory. A science professor at a Christian college asked, "Is there any type of evidence, in any amount, which would convince you that evolution has actually happened, that it's real?"

His answer is equally clear in my memory. After a moment's pause he said, "No. My faith in what I believe is too strong." There were amens and heads that nodded in agreement, but a few of us shared puzzled expressions. While continuing to read conservative literature, I had allowed myself to read more broadly and by then was quite acquainted with a wide array of raw scientific evidence on the topic. Even an occasional student in my high school classes had pointed to weaknesses in conservative explanations of the fossil record.

Among explanations of the sequence of increasing complexity found in the fossil record was something called the "Ecological Zonation Theory." Basically it proposed that the sequence in the fossil record was the result of the Biblical Flood which buried things in sequence according to where they lived, how mobile they were, and how intelligent they were in figuring out how best to escape rising floodwaters. This was all intended to explain in general why mammal and bird fossils are found above (after) reptiles, which are above amphibian, which are above fish, which are above invertebrates. Of course it was noted that apes and humans are both smart and their fossilized remains aren't found until the very upper layers.

I remember a tall, thin student who had more interest in music than science, but who had clear insight. He said this explanation was superficially attractive, but pointed to holes in it. I had to concede to him, "You're right. Various mammals or birds which died in the decades and centuries before the Biblical Flood story could easily have been buried, and the occasional one fossilized in lower layers, yes even down there with the invertebrates." The fact that we don't find scattered glaring exceptions to the obvious sequence spelled trouble to that attempt to explain the fossil record.

Other attempts to explain things have picked on terminology and tried to avoid the evidence for evolution by saying that species can adapt (micro-evolution) but that major change (macro-evolution) hasn't happened. A thorough look at the fossil record of whale evolution from land dwelling mammals provides convincing evidence (follow their limbs, hips, and nostril location in their skulls) that macro-evolution does happen. Some would argue that this is still within mammals, and so it is; but one can also check the evidence for amphibian's ancestors being fish, and the bird-reptile connection.

Other ingenious and sometimes desperate attempts to explain the evidence have been made. One of the most creative I ever heard proposes that the Flood did indeed create a relatively chaotic fossil record like one would expect. But then the devil and his angels saw an opportunity to deceive future generations of man into thinking that there was a pattern which showed a sequence of evolutionary change, so they got right into the messy mud of the Flood aftermath and arranged the fossils. My students have always recognized that we can't prove or disprove that explanation; with a smile we can simply acknowledge that it *is* "possible."

The difference though between possible and probable/logical becomes important. It is possible that I'm nothing more than a worm off in space with a vivid imagination; I imagine my family, my work, even my writing this. It's also possible that you, the reader, are the worm off in space with the vivid imagination; you imagine your family, your work, and reading this. So let's get over what's possible, and begin to really look at what's probable and logical.

I found it troubling that the very accusation leveled at evolutionists, that they form their conclusions ahead of time and selectively look for or create data which supports their theories, turned out to be so overwhelmingly true of my then fellow conservatives. When I finally admitted that I had been part of the reaching and stretching to either ignore or distort the real data, I knew I had to quit teaching science within a conservative Christian school context. Since then I've tried to follow the philosophy of letting the data speak for itself; interpret it in the simplest and most direct way possible. This isn't easy; we *all* have a natural tendency to see and believe what we want to see and believe.

To fight this tendency I have come to a mantra that I think is actually broadly applicable: **Evidence Matters.** And yes, it matters more than what may have been my previously-held, most-cherished beliefs.

This brings me to the first simple truth in this controversial field.

 # 17. The simplest and most direct explanation of the evidence of the fossil record, of comparative molecular biology (both DNA and amino acid sequences), of comparative anatomy, of geographic distribution, and of comparative embryology is evolution by natural selection.

When introducing evolution to classrooms full of public school students who are predominantly from conservative homes, I was careful to help them note exactly what evolution means. It means change over time. I was also careful to note what it does not mean. It does not mean, despite what some insist, anything one way or the other about God. I tried to set them at ease by assuring them that if they don't believe in God, fine, they wouldn't get an argument from me; if they do believe in God, fine, they still wouldn't get an argument from me. What they believe about God is none of my business, and religion wasn't part of what we did in science class. We did science, we did actual evidence.

After going through the various types of evidence showing that indeed things have changed over time (including the mass extinctions and subsequent explosions of diversity) and seeing that things evidently do have ancestral histories, we came to the point of ultimate origins of the first cells. Some of my science colleagues would condemn me for having wimped out, but at this point I tried to leave my individual students with some freedom to believe what they happen to want to about a leap that we can't demonstrate either way (either cells did arise from progressively more complex molecules or they were created). We didn't discuss it in any depth; I simply acknowledged that we can't do real science with "ultimate origins" and so we skipped it. Personally, I'd rather we were helping create a generation which had developed the skill of reasonably interpreting real hard evidence, and that we not *force* young people to buy into the idea that the first cell just happened (abiogenesis and atheism). When forced to that point I think many students just emotionally rebel at the thought and throw the baby (evolution by natural selection) out with the bath water (at least for them a 'possible' case for atheism).

I tried to reassure my students that if they absolutely want and need to have a god, that there is no proof there isn't one. I further informed them that some people, even some with Ph.D.s in science, find personally satisfying and widely creative ways of accepting the evidence for evolution while still believing in a god of some type.

With what I've described in the last few paragraphs some may conclude that I am an advocate of teaching Intelligent Design. I am not. While I don't see a problem in acknowledging that we can't demonstrate hard evidence on how the first cells came about, I see significant short-comings in our level of understanding of natural selection when we resort to saying that all manner of complex organs must have been created from scratch. It may require some major revamping of our preconceptions, but natural selection is an amazing process in itself and there is little serious question, and no real lack of evidence, that it can progressively modify and continue to improve on previous "models." Why not try to understand the mechanism behind a complex process? After all, that is a major part of what science is about.

Our long-ago ancestors accepted many things as magical or divine. If humanity had continued to accept simple or amazing processes as magic, we would be doing without computers, cars, and refrigerators; further, we would still be surviving in crude shelters with no indoor hot running water. Remember that while enjoying a refreshing, warm, and cleansing shower and it adds a little appreciation for the process of scientific inquiry, and for early scientists.

But it does take time to get over certain key preconceptions. Before Nicholas Copernicus worked through the evidence carefully enough to come up with a model that put the sun at the center and explained the motion of the then-known planets, everyone accepted what appeared to be obvious. The Roman Catholic church, conservative Christianity of those early days, wasn't alone in stating that the earth is at the center, that the sun is what moves as it "rises and sets," and that the earth is flat. Shoot, just look around; doesn't that fit the apparent evidence, agree with Scripture, and wasn't it intuitively appealing (just like Intelligent Design) to regular folk and church-goers alike? It took a couple of centuries for this new heliocentric idea to finally gain broad acceptance and for churches and individuals to get over the feeling that their faiths were being swept away.

Although Charles Darwin proposed his idea of evolution by natural selection a century and a half ago now, the public at large has only been really dealing with the idea for about a century. Because people tend to tie the idea of atheism to evolution, and because you can't prove atheism, many continue to resist the overwhelming actual evidence for evolution. It may not be what some want to admit, but the evidence for evolution continues to mount. Scientists well this side of Darwin had no idea how well DNA and amino acid sequences would reveal degrees of relatedness. And the "problem" with absent transitional forms (missing links) is turning out to be a strength as every decade reveals more and more previously absent but newly discovered forms that fit in where predicted. Still, that doesn't change the fact that it is going to take some time to accept evolution the way we eventually accepted the earth not being at the center, and to get over being threatened by the idea.

(If you find yourself resistant to, but a little puzzled by and curious about the notion of evolution, I would suggest you read the cover article in the November 2004 *National Geographic*. It is not anti-God, and it does a good job of giving the reader an overview of the evidence.)

During the time it takes for our culture to work this through, we might do well to be a little bit patient with each other. But while we're patient, we still need to be careful. Blending religious belief with science, especially in the classroom, is a mistake at least in part because this action arrests a fundamental part of what science is about: the search to understand natural mechanisms. Keeping religion-based assertions out of science instruction not only should place some constraints on the science teacher who happens to be an Evangelical Christian (he shouldn't push his belief in God), it also places some constraints on the science teacher who happens to be a convinced atheist (he shouldn't push his belief that there is no god).

In summary, my last simple truth related to science education.

 # 18. Intelligent Design might be taught in a philosophy class, but it should not be taught as part of 'science' because it short-cuts the key scientific process of seeking to understand natural mechanisms and it introduces articles of "faith" where "questioning" should be standard procedure.

It is too bad that issues like this have to end up in court, but if we make it another couple centuries, I think people will look back on the uproar rather like we look back on the fight over whether the sun or the earth is at the center. I've been reassured to see the collective wisdom of the voters in Dover, Pennsylvania, (November, 2005) who, despite many of them holding religious beliefs, spoke clearly at the ballot box in saying that they can take care of religious beliefs outside of the science classroom. Yes, let science be science.

Most importantly in the big picture, whatever we each take as articles of faith, let's not mistake them for science, and let's take them with sufficient humility so as to not drag ourselves or our nation into wasting resources or engaging in cultural conflict or war to prop up our particular beliefs. I like to think that good science education can help us avoid this type of waste and conflict. If we apply the mantra that **Evidence Matters,** even more than our cherished preconceptions, to any potential war situation, it may well make a difference in our decisions on that conflict.

Chapter 9.

Too Many Topics – Not Enough Time: (Immigration Policy, Soft and Spoiled, Energy, and Affirmative Action)

If I have upset members of the "right" in my previous chapters, by the end of this chapter I'll be taking arrows from two directions because I know that a lot of what I say in this section will upset those on the "left." So be it. Again, my hope is that we in the middle will increasingly speak up and limit the influence of the squeaky extremes, and that we will question beliefs on both ends, and logically think things through.

In areas like these I don't bring any particular professional or experiential expertise; rather, I will take what I consider to be a common sense approach. Obviously there is room for debate. I speak up, despite knowing I will take some fire, simply because these are important areas which I believe will affect the long-term stability and strength of our nation.

Immigration

The current situation of lax border enforcement and lax "legal laborer/legal employer" enforcement is a long-term recipe for disaster. Let's cut to the chase. Business seems addicted to access to cheap labor, but illegal cheap labor is a problem, and it's a problem largely of our own making. We Americans – from home-owners with yard work, to farmers with crops to harvest, to business owners large and small – have wanted to do things on the cheap without regard to broad consequences or basic legality. It is therefore "we" who have had the largest part in making the bed we are now complaining about lying in. Business throws around the excuse that if they couldn't hire such cheap labor, the price of all kinds of products and services would have to be passed on to consumers. Of course they would, but what's wrong with that? I believe that our economy can absorb reality.

The spin-off costs of illegal immigration are wide-ranging and enormous. Why should tax paying American citizens support the health care, welfare, and education of people who have no right to **be** here, let alone a right to those services? We should note here however, that if we continue to turn a blind eye to their coming and working here because we like being able to hire cheap labor, then we are users if we don't let them benefit from the economy they help support.

It's also worth noting that we probably do have the necessary laborers-in-the-making right here at home. If not every one of our American students choose to succeed on the university prep track, shouldn't there be a demand in the economy for homegrown laborers, and shouldn't we be able and willing to pay the lowest end of our labor force a wage sufficient to support a decent, if decidedly non-luxurious, living?

Will it be easy to wake up, smell the coffee, and start enforcing all relevant aspects of legal immigration? This obviously must include not only border enforcement but also strong penalties for Americans trying to hire on the cheap.

No, it won't be easy, but I believe that in the long run it will turn out to be worth it.

Interestingly, while there may be some in the Hispanic community who feel that there is racism behind any move to tighten illegal immigration, it is members of the legal Hispanic community (who have as much right to be here as any of us; many of whom **are** American citizens) who have the most to gain by enforcing the legality of being here. For starters, wages for the less skilled would no longer be depressed by the ready availability of workers who have no legal recourse against unfair employers. This benefit to the legal Hispanic community is broadly true under normal circumstances, but other benefits most people would be unaware of could become significant should we come under extreme circumstances.

Let me illustrate extreme circumstances. I have lived where resource competition and economic survival stress merged with previously low-level ethnic tension and reached a breaking point, and it was horrific. Obviously I refer to Rwanda and what happened in 1994. Before making the point I want to, let me assure you that I am well aware that the chaos that exploded around us there was multi-factorial, and that because our whole country is much more educated, we are at substantially less risk of degenerating into that degree of madness. Also before going on to the heart of the matter, because it is too easy for time and distance to fog our memories, allow me to remind you that in only about three months approximately three quarters of a million people were 'eliminated' (at that time that was almost 10% of their population).

Here is a significant part of how this happened there. Rwanda was a country of eight million people, with not even a half million of those people living in significant villages, the eight major towns, and the capital city <u>combined</u>!

actually THINKING

It was the most evenly spread rural population-base I have even seen. It was as if a giant hand holding a salt shaker of huts had shaken them across the countryside; you could have literally hit a golf ball from any hut to some other huts. While there was not the abject poverty found in huge cities in developing countries, few had any luxuries. Nearly everyone lived hand-to-mouth off the little land they culti- vated. And, as of 1994, the average woman was still having over seven children in her lifetime. As the population had boomed since the 1950s, families had simply progressively carved up the land they owned among their many children. A basic economic survival resource, land, was reaching a critical stress point.

Add to that basic scenario the following: a severely undereducated population (more subject to manipulation), a level of political stress from attempts to move toward multiparty democracy, and politicians more than willing to exploit an existing low level of ethnic suspicion and mis- trust, and turn those into raw fear that it was either kill or be killed. Suddenly whole communities were whipped up to the point where fear had morphed into animalistic killer instinct combined with uniquely human hatred. Oh, there were noteworthy islands of sanity, heroism, and even self- sacrifice. But basically, other societal dividing lines – from church membership, to neighborhood, to marriage, to work association – dissolved amidst ethnic tensions gone wild.

In America it is jobs, not land, which could most likely become the basic economic survival resource. Are there various ethnic stresses? Certainly. If uncontrolled demand for, acceptance of, and movement of illegal immigration continues, and then the economy takes a dive serious enough to turn our current recession into a genuine depres- sion, we could be in for some rough and shameful times. Again, I firmly believe that our overall level of education

118

would make us much less susceptible to manipulation by any crazy politician or radical member of the media, but I have seen enough violence in my time to have a healthy fear of what humans can devolve into when pushed to their breaking point. I am sure that there are unnumbered millions of Americans who made sure to have friendly casual conversations with fellow-Americans of Middle Eastern descent following 9-11; we wanted them to know that we viewed them like any other American. Unfortunately there were also scattered cases in which some fearful, reactionary, and bigoted citizen used the justified anti-terrorist environment as an excuse to lash out at some who just "looked" like the wrong ethnic group.

I trust that the overwhelming majority of any side of ethnic stress in America would take the side of right, and not participate in any hate-based intimidation or killing. But should we let uncontrolled immigration add to the various stresses that will be part of life when we do have economic tough times at a broad and deep level? And might I add to my fellow-Americans who happen to be of Hispanic origin, if you take the lead in calling for realistic, modernized, and *enforced* immigration policies, besides benefiting the most, won't you also have the most effective voice?

It may well be worth noting that the most efficient and effective aspect of enforcement probably isn't simply border security. If we really step up in our expectations of each other to always and only hire laborers who are legally here, and we back that up with *serious* penalties for doing otherwise, we would find millions of illegals actually heading back home voluntarily because they are out of work and can't find a job. Then we would find the tide of new illegals drying up in a hurry; the lack of demand on this side would do more to stop the flow than anything else. It appears now in 2010 that some are seriously advocating this approach;

others are advocating large-scale amnesty. Watch closely. One will dry up this problem for the long haul, the other will encourage further illegal border crossing in the hopes of some future amnesty.

At the bottom line,

 # 19. The long-term economic and social health of our nation will be better off if we work to strictly limit immigration to *legal* immigration.

In the big picture, the illegal immigration problem here and the atrocities committed in Rwanda both have to do with uncontrolled population growth. Not only is our lack of "legal laborer" enforcement creating a magnet on our side of the border, but the continued steep population growth rate in Mexico creates emigration pressure there. I'm not saying it is our business to do something about on-the-ground family planning policy 'enforcement' in Mexico or any other developing nation, but I do believe that we need to be conscious of the problem, and begin to affect attitudes.

Addressing the global population growth situation may well be one of the keys to humanity's survival for the next 250 years. If we make it that far without degenerating into chaos, we can make it much, much deeper in time. One could easily connect a broad range of problems, from war to water pollution, from disease epidemic risk to global warming, all to the population situation, but that would be a needless side-track from the point at hand. We must also keep in mind that it is too easy for us in America to see the population challenge as something we have already controlled at home, and have no affect on in the world abroad.

Though we can't and shouldn't get involved in enforcement of family planning, we can constructively encourage the circumstances in which population stability tends to happen. Rather than expressing our incredulity at impoverished people having large families only to watch many of their children suffer and die, it is worth noting that we in the West benefited from reduced death rates (especially among the very young) *before* we brought birth rates down. That bears repeating: death rates come down first, then birth rates come down (as people develop confidence that their few children have every likelihood of surviving, not only childhood, but into their old age).

What leads to low death rates? Some might think of modern health care systems, but a much more fundamental prerequisite could be termed basic quality of life. If you reflect on that for a moment you realize it encompasses employment, education, and the whole economic infrastructure.

As I mentioned in the introduction to Part III of this book, although we must accept the competitive nature of economic survival in the world, it is nevertheless true that **what is good for us in the long run necessarily takes into consideration what is good for humanity in a global sense.** They go together. It takes thinking beyond how to out-compete our fellow humans.

Before commenting further on what we can do to help create population stabilizing circumstances, I am going to point out one thing that has had an adverse affect on bringing population growth into check. As a public health worker in Rwanda I made family planning a priority. I very quickly found out that 'access' wasn't as big a problem as 'attitudes and beliefs.' There were local 'traditional' reasons for resistance to family planning, but in the middle of Africa the most frequently voiced objection was the Catholic church's official position against it.

I'm not Catholic bashing; I'm simply pointing out that

a Western-based influence is making the global population situation, especially in developing nations, a bigger and longer-lasting problem. The same influence is significant in Mexico. What can we do about it? Regular citizens might feel like answering "nothing." I hope though, that we never underestimate the power of persistent people. Yes, the Vatican is ever so slow to change, but look at what average American Catholics have long since put into practice in their own lives. They have seen for several generations that "Be fruitful and multiply" has been more than followed, and that other Biblical guidance also calls us to take good care of children and avoid needless suffering. Imagine millions of regular Catholics taking the lead in putting grass-roots pressure on the Vatican from within the church. Personally, I have to be hopeful.

Other aspects of creating the right circumstances for population stability most obviously include raising the quality of life and thereby lowering death rates (the first step). How do we most effectively engage ourselves in raising the quality of life in developing nations? It might be surprising to some, but hand-out aid is not the best way. One of the hardest lessons I had to learn in Rwanda (and we can see here too) is that aid has to be channeled carefully and wisely or it will create dependence, not initiative and independence. We need to ensure open and fair trade. We need to invest where free and open markets make it possible. (One more of my highly recommended readings is *The Opportunity*, by Richard Haass. Again, I have condensed and simplified the point here to a tremendous degree; this whole work is a very worthwhile read!) In summary, we need to act with the knowledge that **the long-term good of the poor in developing countries *is* tied to our long-term good.**

Having dealt broadly with the global population situation, it will be constructive to return briefly to the immigration issue directly. It should be obvious that there eventually needs to be an end to even legal immigration. If the earth doesn't have an infinite carrying capacity, neither does America; population stability at some point must be a good thing.

For millennia we have expanded human impact into 'nature,' with the rate of that expansion accelerating tremendously in the last century. Yet ultimately it is nature, living things, which keeps earth in livable balance and sustains us. If we encroach forever, we do so at our own peril.

And if we need unskilled labor or highly skilled specialists, so does the rest of the world; and we darn well ought to commit to living within our means and letting supply and demand work its magic inside our borders. To continue to depend on importing laborers or specialists is to let ourselves stay dependent on a crutch which will ultimately cripple us.

An objection, almost certainly held by most politicians, to drawing down *all* immigration to the zero point is that actually achieving population stability would have a significant impact on the economy. We are addicted to the idea of economic *growth*. One of the basic engines in the economy is home construction. An ever-growing population means continuing demand for more housing. To end population growth would mean that new home construction would cool down to a significantly lower 'replacement/maintenance' level. The relative disappearance of the construction engine to the economy would be a significant factor in diminishing or ending economic growth. So what? Ultimately don't we need to shift our thinking from 'growth' to 'sustainability'? Quality of life isn't dependent on growth; in fact, in the long run it is a focus on sustainability which can maintain quality of life.

A related economic impact of population stability

would be that in the absence of constant demand for more housing, property values for houses and land would stabilize too. That's not a bad thing, but it would take some adjustment in our thinking and investment strategies because we are so used to the idea of our properties gaining value as the years role on.

On so many issues in the world today we would do well to look in the mirror and remind ourselves that, "It's about sustainability stupid," it's not all about me, now. (For a fascinating and thorough look at one aspect of sustainability which each of us can quickly begin to apply in our own lives, consider reading Michael Pollan's *The Omnivor's Dilemma*.")

Soft and Spoiled

A recurring theme in this book is the need for the heretofore too silent middle to become more active in setting public policy. In this section, I'm not sure the public policy aspect applies to curing or reversing the imbalance of the sense of entitlement vs. practical reality, but the attitudes and actions of thinking middle-Americans certainly do apply. Though my concerns about our being so spoiled that we will fall apart from within focus somewhat on today's youth, this problem definitely crosses generations.

Unfortunately, too many young people today have a sense that life "should" continue to get easier, no matter that they don't want to work hard to make it happen. Too many don't want to put serious effort into school, but they still want to find a high paying job. Too many have no idea of how hard life was for those who endured the depression and World War II, or how hard life still is in most of the world.

If circumstances drastically changed, I believe a new generation of tough survivors would emerge. But what if life doesn't suddenly change? What if we just gradually drift into ever greater personal and national debt and into deeper trade deficits? The possibilities for our economy and culture are scary.

Even among an older generation of Baby Boomers and their parents who should have some closer connection to the real meaning of sacrifice and hardship, unrealistic expectations of entitlement can have broad and damaging affects on our sustainability. People bemoan the supposed shame of some having to choose between paying the heating bill and affording the multiple prescription drugs that keep them ticking. What sacred law or reasonable principle says that we as individuals or as a whole society can or should afford the potentially unlimited costs of keeping us alive? Is this question even more applicable when many of the chronic diseases that so burden us economically are often self-inflicted by poorly chosen and soft lifestyles?

As I suggested at the beginning of this section, I'm not sure there are policy solutions to these problems. There are though, attitudinal and action solutions. Take for example the problem of agricultural harvest being dependent on illegal labor. I have heard it asserted for decades now that if not for illegal migrant laborers, many fruit crops would just fall off the trees and rot. This is likely at least partially, if not wholly, true. The irony is that this is true while there are not-too-distant cities with numerous people on various welfare or unemployment programs.

Before we urban middle-Americans get too comfortable pointing fingers, perhaps we ought to ask ourselves if we have able-bodied pre-teens and teens who don't have full-time summer jobs. Imagine that farmers and orchardists had web-sites where I could sign myself and two of my kids up for a week or two "working vacation." For urban kids everywhere, a week or two of physical labor in harvesting a valuable crop would probably be a positive, profitable, and character-building experience. I suspect that we have the necessary labor force sitting around thinking that life just happens for them. Is this one simple partial-solution meant to imply that the whole problem of agricultural harvest and our softness and dependence on illegal labor could be easily solved? Not at all. It is meant as an example of actually recognizing a problem, and then taking steps to address it. Often large solutions can be composed of many different partial-solutions. Where there's a will, there's a way.

Simply put,

20. The combination of exporting our jobs and importing our laborers while expecting to maintain our lifestyle is non-sustainable pie-in-the-sky. We must re-value hard work and re-evaluate our expectations.

Having mentioned both illegal and legal immigration in the previous section, I feel compelled to point out the connection between those and this section on our soft and spoiled status. What drives illegal immigration? Both employers falling for the temptation to save a buck while ignoring the law, and the fact that employers too often can't find enough willing laborers. Why can't they? Because too many homegrown citizens are too lazy to do the hard labor.

So if softness and laziness is behind our dependence on importing unskilled and illegal labor to fill tough jobs, what is behind our dependence on importing highly skilled labor like pharmacists, engineers, doctors, and nurses? Indeed, why aren't we producing enough of these highly skilled and well-paid laborers to meet our own needs? Why don't more young people see the open demand, great pay, and bright careers open to them? Well actually, young people are *aware* of these possibilities. So why aren't they stepping up to the plate of opportunity? To some degree it is because it takes a lot of hard work to get there, it takes seeing past instant gratification, and it requires not taking the lazy way out. I say 'to some degree' because in many of these highly skilled professions, some of the graduate/ professional schools turn away nine applicants for every one that they accept. Granted, some of these applicants haven't put in the hard work to make themselves a highly competitive candidate. A substantial part of the problem though is that we as a society haven't built the educational infrastructure of more medical, pharmacy, and engineering schools; the low-tax mantra has been shortsighted. More on our financial priorities and failure to take the broad and long view in the next chapter.

Wow, so laziness is behind our dependence on import-ing both unskilled and highly skilled labor. Those twin dependencies are rather like a capable person allowing himself to walk with some form of crutch just because it's temporarily easier. Fine, it works for now, but someday our weak legs will need to carry our own weight, and we may well fall flat on our faces. We simply shouldn't be so dependent on these two crutches to keep our economy and country going!

No, this isn't an anti-immigrant diatribe. We are nearly all immigrants. But a propped-up economy is still that, and it is still non-sustainable. We can't absorb the unwanted from overpopulated countries forever, and we shouldn't be the cause continuing the brain drain that many countries have suffered for too long. It may be politically unpopular in the short-term, but we should turn off the tap of im-migration of all types and learn to meet our own needs for labor of all types across the board.

The details of the rate at which to turn off the tap would need a careful look, but the bottom-line need must not get lost in the details. We would indeed *have* to become more willing to work as a whole population. We would have to raise the value given to hard physical labor. We would have to quit giving a free pass to the freeloaders in our midst. (This does not label or disparage those in legitimate need of societal support; it simply recognizes the reality that we've been too patient with those unwilling to work, and it must end.) We would have to buy into the idea that some forms of hard work (education) can have delayed gratification. And we really have to shift from the 'growth' mentality to a 'sustainability' mentality. But all of this, my friend, is so doable.

Energy

Some things are so obvious they don't even merit bold print. There is not an infinite supply of fossil fuels. With continued economic growth in much of the developing world, the demand for petroleum is increasing, and is going to continue to increase. Limited supply plus increasing demand mean ever-increasing prices. What's the solution? Increasing efficiency and utilization of an array of energy forms like solar, wind, tide, geothermal, and hydrogen fuel cells will help. Much more space could be dedicated to emphasizing the importance of developing these alternative energy sources, but I'm not going to spend time discussing things which I think most of us already agree on. I must point out though the one potentially large-scale energy source which we have been neglecting most: nuclear energy has been put on hold for longer than we can realistically afford.

Fear from experiences like Three Mile Island and Chernobyl has kept us with the brakes on, but we simply can't stay that way. Some say, "But we'd be poisoning ourselves." My reply is that we have at least a very high probability of containing nuclear waste indefinitely, and right now we are living with more than a high probability of slowly poisoning our atmosphere by burning fossil fuels. Atmospheric Carbon dioxide (CO_2) levels have climbed for every single year in the last half century; there are no maybes to what we **are** doing to the air that sustains all life. Unless we suddenly find ourselves with a much smaller global population which demands much less energy, we must face the fact that nuclear is the only option that meets the scale of demand that we have on our hands.

In case you are one of the dwindling few who still try to shrug at climbing CO_2 levels and what you consider to be the climate change "controversy," please temporarily set aside your belief, and check the following facts. For CO_2 level itself, Google the Keeling Curve. Verify that CO_2 acts as an effective heat trap (any number of sources, but for a history-rich one, check www.aip.org/history/climate/co2.htm). Further, just think about this: in 1930 the human population reached two billion, and no generation of people had ever lived through a doubling of the population. Remember that we had hit our first billion in 1800. Those born before 1930 who are still alive have now lived through more than a tripling of the population! Now ask yourself, how much combustion of any fuel did the average person among those living in 1800 do in their lifetime? Now think of how much the average person burns today (be sure to picture the indirect, not in-person, burning we do beyond driving our cars and heating our homes; remember, energy-intense products include aluminum cans, plastic, and innumerable common daily items). Can we seriously be the least bit surprised that we have raised a significant atmospheric component to levels higher than ice-core samples show going back nearly the last half million years? Further, can we be surprised that this historically high CO_2 level would have some significant consequences on other aspects of our atmosphere and ocean (temperature and pH)? As Bill Cosby might say, "Come on people!" Look at concrete evidence and think; don't just believe what you have always believed.

Before going on with a few more points with regard to nuclear energy, I must point out several common-sense-related particulars with regard to some of the resistance to taking a serious look at climate change. Skeptics have recently pointed to the lack of ever-increasing atmospheric temperature data points from around the world. Well, if we keep in mind a few basics from high school physics or chemistry, this lack of quickly upwardly spiraling *atmospheric* temperature shouldn't surprise us.

One of these basics is the exceptionally high *specific heat* of water. Remember that this is the amount of energy it takes to change the temperature of a given mass of a substance (often expressed in calories to change 1 gram by 1 degree Celsius). It is water's high specific heat that gives coastal towns their relatively warm winters and their relatively cool summers, as compared to towns of the same latitude much further inland. (Compare Seattle, Washington, to Bismarck, North Dakota.) Water, on the massive scale of our oceans, serves as a tremendous heat-sink. Even if the atmosphere could "try" to raise its temperature by several degrees, it would quickly loose that heat to the oceans where that temperature-change would "disappear" into a small fraction of the change that the atmosphere would have shown. Water, because of its high specific heat, acts as a tremendous shock-absorber, smoothing out any little bumps in the road of temperature-change. Still, those fractions of degrees change in our oceans will add up.

A second basic concept to remember is what keeps even the temperatures of our oceans from relatively quickly registering more change than they do. Remember the energy transfers in *phase change*? If you have an amount of ice at 32 degrees F, it can absorb a large amount of energy before it ends up as liquid, still at 32 degrees F. Now apply this to what is going on with ice on a global level. Greenland and Antarctica have over seven million cubic *miles* of ice. Then there are glaciers in the Himalayas, Alps, Andes, Rockies, and much of Alaska. Ice melting in any of these places absorbs a tremendous amount of energy from the atmosphere, keeping it from showing much in the way of sharp or steady temperature climb. Further, this newly-melted cold water enters our oceans, keeping them from showing as much temperature change as the ocean would register from all the energy it absorbs directly from the atmosphere. And make no mistake – ice-melt is happening to a much greater extent than atmospheric temperatures are climbing. (If you haven't read the article on Greenland in the June, 2010 issue of *National Geographic*, read it. We all know that *National Geographic* doesn't do cheap or shallow sensationalism; they do thorough and quality journalism.)

I've written the previous few paragraphs to help us understand why global temperatures aren't spiking like the skeptics say they should if global warming were real. The shock-absorbing role of our oceans and of melting ice can keep us complacently pointing to the lack of sharp and continuous atmospheric temperature changes – but it shouldn't!

I've avoided the interruption of numerous source citations to allow for uninterrupted reading, and because it is so easy to verify or to question any assertion today. Please, do your own homework on any of the above, particularly on the rate and geographical pervasiveness of ice-melt in recent years. You don't have to be a "believer" in global warming; just look at the hard facts from a variety of verifiable and objective sources like NASA, facts that are as precise as modern satellite technology and on-the-ground measurements make possible. Indeed, question, think, check, analyze, but don't just *believe*.

Now back to nuclear energy. Modern nuclear technology has been engineered to be very reliable and virtually fail-safe. I know, never say never, but it really can be incredibly safe. Add to that safety the basic pragmatic considerations of energy demand, low environmental impact, and long-term low cost and we might as well get back to developing these generating facilities *now* rather than waiting until we are truly desperate.

 # 21. Nuclear generated power is an essential part of our long-term energy viability, and the sooner, and the more of it, the better.

(For the still-skeptical I must make one more book recommendation at this point. Read Gwyneth Cravens' *Power to Save the World: the Truth about Nuclear Energy.* Note that she was at one time strongly anti-nuclear, and her research, undertaken with an antinuclear bias, changed her position. This just happens to be an example of thinking and evidence overcoming a prior belief.)

As to drilling in the Arctic National Wildlife Refuge (ANWR), Alaska, the real issue might well be that of timing. Some day we may absolutely need to drill because oil prices and our level of dependence on foreign oil will demand it. To some degree though, the further we can put it off, the better. I don't know how long it takes to get from agreeing, "Okay, we need to do this" to getting oil on line, but I imagine five years could do it. ANWR then can act like a long-term strategic reserve. Exploit it too soon and we just continue our "live for today; tomorrow whatever" mentality. And then in some real tomorrow we have less of an economic buffer from what eventually could become the last major reserve on earth. To begin concrete plans to drill there will also have the negative effect of decreasing our level of commitment and urgency in improving the technology and mass use of other alternatives.

Affirmative Action

Some might say that this is none of my business, and others might ask what this has to do with anything. Well, I bring it up because, though minor, it is almost a reflection of some small issues that can be destabilizing to our broader society over the long haul.

Was affirmative action a necessary and good thing? Absolutely yes. Is it still? Possibly. Will it be indefinitely? Certainly not. The shameful blot that slavery and racism, both individual and institutional, cast on our national heritage is regrettable and undeniable. Affirmative action was an essential part of attempting to level the playing field of opportunity for which America stands. But I can easily imagine a day when talented and motivated African-Americans and other minorities would want to be recognized for their drive and achievement without any possibility of a perceived asterisk by it.

 # 22. Affirmative action has been a good thing, but its end should be in sight.

The question then is one of timing. Have we reached that day? Perhaps, and perhaps not quite. But should we within the next quarter century? One would think surely. This is really a debate that can most effectively be led by African-Americans and other minorities themselves, and many of them would stand to loose a stigma and gain one of the final steps to real equality. True equality of opportunity is one of the foundations on which the long-term stability of our nation and culture rests.

Post-script on Race Relations

Having dealt with illegal immigration and affirmative action, in which Hispanics and African-Americans are naturally interested racial subgroups, I feel compelled to add a few clarifying remarks. The remarks I add though, are very definitely directed to each and every ethnic subgroup, whether they be Korean, Indian, or White.

An important question to ask ourselves is: Am I most interested in protecting and promoting people of my own ethnic group, or am I most interested in protecting and promoting American values? I will add some more pointed questions to this in a moment, but for now let's start by reminding ourselves of what core American values are.

Two simple words sum it up: freedom and equality. We have many freedoms, and among the most important of these is speech. Whatever our other differences on various values, we are free to discuss and debate them without fear because of freedom of speech. When we refer to equality, we all know we are not referring to the enforced "equality" of Communism, but to equality of opportunity.

As complimentary as freedom and equality are to each other, they still impose logical limits on each other. In order to avoid keeping a permanent underclass, or creating new ones, or de facto keeping a permanent ruling class, the freedom to pursue and keep wealth must be tempered by the American value of equality of opportunity. Notice that implied in equality of opportunity is the very basic idea of fairness. The unfortunate history of racism, whose aftermath we are still overcoming, illustrates the need to limit certain aspects of freedom in education, business contracts, and such, in order to advance the value of equality of opportunity, the idea of fairness. Yes, affirmative action was absolutely necessary.

What about today? I will first ask a pointed question to American Hispanics. On the question of legal vs. illegal immigration, do you favor ideas like blanket amnesty for illegals? Do you hope for continued weak borders? If so, why? If you find in your heart an inclination to favor policies (or the lack of policy) which favor your ethnic group over the basic American value of fairness, are you being an American or, in a way, racist? If you find yourself uncomfortable with the question and with your initial response, it is not hopeless. With rational analysis, with objective thinking, we all can work through beliefs which we may not even have realized we held. Progress is possible.

My second pointed question goes to Whites. Can we recognize that the value of equality of opportunity made affirmative action a necessary positive action, and that we alone shouldn't be the only group to decide when it becomes unnecessary? Whether or not we harbor some degree of racism in our individual hearts may be best answered by asking ourselves if we would be completely comfortable, or not, with a child of ours marrying a person from another ethnic group.

The last pointed questions go to African-Americans. If you have cultivated in your children a respect and appreciation for education as an 'opportunity,' do you think they will need any special consideration? Does indefinitely continuing the policy of affirmative action not ultimately go against the basic value of equality of opportunity?

For several generations young American men and women of all races have fought side-by-side in a number of wars to defend American values. Can't we all reach the same point here at home? Shouldn't we be able to stand for these values even if it means taking a stand against some of our own ethnic group? Then we as individuals will know that we are truly <u>American</u>, and not at all racist. The more we are truly American, in values not in ethnicity, the stronger and more just America will be. And the stronger and more just we are in the world, the better our chances of cultivating a stable, secure, and potentially steadily improving world.

As I have watched our society respond to having elected an African-American as president, deal with a recession, and struggle with unresolved illegal immigration issues, my concerns over the possibility that we could degenerate into ugliness haven't subsided. We will have internal competition for resources of many kinds, including jobs; that's reality. We can choose though, how we respond. We must do everything within our control to set justifiable policies in place so as to not give excuses for radical action to crazy people. We must have the courage to be tolerant of everything except intolerance.

There are already hate-mongers within our midst. I see finger-pointing emails circulate; I hear some talk radio hosts spout nonsense; I read articles about the increase in hate-groups of various types. All of this should make us pause. We don't have to react like fearful and easily manipulated illiterate people. We can and must question beliefs that are divisive and destructive. We can and must be up to the task. We must stand for right, for freedom, for equality of opportunity; we must give no quarter to bigotry and prejudice aimed from *any* group toward *any* other group.

Chapter 10.

Wishful Thinking:
Low Taxes and Great Services
vs. A Balanced Budget

The need to begin thinking beyond what we want now has already been mentioned, and that notion is most applicable right in the middle of a discussion of taxes and spending, of entitlements and reasonable expectations, and of who benefits and how from our collective purse. This is also a prime topic on which to put genuine effort into placing thinking above simply believing. In the *very* near future we must move from *discussing* taxes and spending to *doing something* about them. Economists much more familiar with the details than I have been stressing that the long-term economic health of our nation depends on getting our financial house in order. The question I will look at is "How?"

Many have no doubt noted the irony of conservatives like then President Bush calling for increased "volunteerism" in constructive community activities while also calling for larger tax cuts for the very richest segment of our society. Sometimes the degree to which the far right succeeded in duping so many of us amazes me. The subtle spin created among the very wealthy segment of the far right has wound up getting the entire right, including some surprisingly lower working class folks, to chant the "cut taxes; they're punitive" mantra. We'll see through this veneer shortly.

I don't know many truly wealthy folks, but I do remember one of them complaining off-handedly that he pays more than his share of taxes, and all the while doesn't benefit from *any* government program. My reply was direct: "You benefit from the # 1 government program: providing for and ensuring societal stability. If not for the stability around you, you couldn't have accumulated your wealth. And if not for continued stability around you, you won't be able to maintain your wealth." After a pause he nodded, but went on to note the degree of waste that happens in the government's distribution of other benefits. The "average" wealthy citizen isn't duped so much as unrecognizing of the reality and true extent of their benefits.

The average hard-working middle class citizen bought into the low-tax mantra of the right because the tax-and-spend mentality of the left had gone too far. That's legitimate. We were duped though into buying the idea that, no matter what societal service is sacrificed, lower is always better when it comes to taxes. Further, we were duped into believing that whatever someone can earn in a free market economy, they "deserve" it. Be patient now, I'm not a commie, and I will explain.

I cannot and will not argue that they "**don't** deserve" what they get any more than someone can argue that they "**do** deserve" what they get. I believe in the free market economy, and if professional athletes, corporate CEOs, high-powered attorneys, and movie stars happen to be able to command a lot in our system, so be it. It is simply what they **can** get, and "deserving" it isn't for us to question **or** to concede. But for us to bow like humble lambs and say that they shouldn't pay more in taxes is being duped.

 # 23. Having a higher tax rate, a progressive and substantially higher one, for the extremely wealthy isn't confiscatory or punitive. Rather, it simply has them pay disproportionately into supporting the free enterprise system from which they benefit disproportionately.

Despite what some may be muttering at this point, I am not a tax-and-spend liberal. I know very well that communism, carried to its extreme, will suffocate itself like a beached whale. I am pointing out though that capitalism, carried to its extreme, will dismember nearly all of its participants like a bunch of chomping beetles enclosed in too small a container. Yes, on one hand we need our true fiscal conservatives acting as our constant watchdogs against government waste (and corruption!); but on the other hand we must recognize that we need to continue to tweak capitalism to bring out the broad best in our society. Despite the elitist mantra that a lower tax rate for the wealthy is good for the economy, there is nothing economically good about increasing deficits and certainly not about our ever-growing debt.

Another common complaint from the right with regard to higher taxes on the wealthy is that it is redistributing the wealth. A quick look at the trends in percent of taxes paid and the incomes of the richest and the rest makes that complaint laughable. Look it up; I will be using Congressional Budget Office data you can check at http://www.cbo.gov/doc.cfm?index=8885. Those on the right who complain about redistribution won't like the facts, but we have been progressively redistributing the wealth, **from** the 'rest' **to** the 'richest' ever since about 1980. In 1980 the top 1% took in 9.1% of pretax income, and the bottom 80% of us took in about 54.2%. By 2005 the top 1% took in 18.1% of pretax income, virtually doubling their take. By 2005 the bottom 80% of us had dropped to 44.9% of pretax income, *actually THINKING*

losing almost 10% of the 1980 share. (see Table 1C at the CBO website) Yes, we have been doing a grand job of redistributing the wealth, from the middle class to the richest.

As if this picture of shifting wealth isn't bad enough, it gets worse when you look closer. When you consider how much income people can generate by simply using the wealth they happen to already have, it is impressive. I have condensed the table below from a Congressional Budget Office table shown in Appendix B.

Share of Capital Income Flowing to Households in Various Income Categories

	Bottom 80%	Top 1%
1980	24.5%	35.6%
1985	25.8%	39.7%
1990	24.4%	39.7%
1995	21.0%	43.2%
2000	17.1%	49.1%
2005	12.2%	58.6%

Stop and think about these data. The relative ability of the top 1% to put their wealth to work to earn still more income has increased by over 20%. Meanwhile the relative ability of the bottom 80% of us to generate income by putting our money to work has been cut in half. None of this is an accident. The tax policies that we accept as handed down from our leaders, including tax cuts for the wealthiest, led to this trend. Do we actually want this trend to continue? Do we really think this trend is justified?

Speaking of trends, a picture paints a thousand words, so check this graph taken from William Domhoff's *Who Rules America?* (http://sociology.ucsc.edu/whorulesamerica/power/wealth.html).

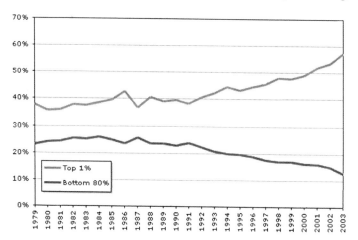

Figure 5: Share of capital income earned by top 1% and bottom 80%, 1979-2003 (From Shapiro & Friedman, 2006.)

Yes, we'll still hear complaints like, "Just 1% of us pay over a quarter of the taxes, and only 20% of us pay over two thirds of the taxes. That's just ridiculous." Well, look broadly through the CBO data, Table 1B and 1C, and you realize that the reply is, "The 1% who pay a quarter of the taxes are taking in almost one fifth of all income, and over half of the capital income. Further, the 20% who are paying two thirds of the taxes are taking in 55% of all income, and over 85% of capital income." The whining about redistributive tax policy milking the wealthy to favor the middle class or poor should end; the data show that for over a quarter century it has clearly been a case of redistributing the wealth from the middle class to the wealthy. Is that conscionable, or constructive?

One of the ironies in this discussion is the blatant disrespect that many of the mega-wealthy have for the common man. CEO's who accept government bailouts for their troubled corporations, and then accept and hand out bonuses to the tune of millions seem to have neither conscience nor respect for the everyday hardworking Joe. This disrespect was made clear by Pat Buchanan when, speaking in an October 2008 edition of *The McLaughlin Group*, he said in effect, "Obama's proposed tax increase on those earning over $250,000 is a penalty on the ***successful***." What does he imply about every nurse, electrician, truck driver, teacher, plumber, clerk, sales manager, research assistant, and the majority of even doctors, attorneys, accountants, engineers, small business owners, farmers, and computer specialists? Interestingly, not one of Buchanan's fellow panel members pointed out his labeling of under-$250K-earners as falling short of *successful*.

Getting back to tax rates – let's face the reality that in order to close the deficit and to begin paying down the debt (rather than simply passing an ever-larger debt on to our kids and grandkids) we must not only spend less from government coffers, we must also take in more in taxes. No, that's not politically popular, but it is a grownup approach to managing money, be it personal or collective. So, if we can begin to view taxes as 'the responsible thing' and not a 'bad thing' or a 'good thing,' who is it who can help the most? The answer is obvious, and it is not an injustice. If a wealthy person will still have his nice lifestyle after paying his sliding-scale greater tax, I would suggest that he indeed could feel patriotic for doing more to fix a serious problem.

Remember a comment in "Soft and Spoiled" on how part of our problem with not being able to produce enough doctors, engineers, and other professionals, is that we haven't continued to develop the institutional infrastructure? Well, what pays to build university research facilities, hospitals, and so many things whose "return" to society can take decades? Yes, taxes are just the responsible and, viewed broadly and long-term, wise thing to do. Tax payers, from top to bottom, can and should feel patriotic.

Whether or not you are convinced as you read this, I must refer you to a remarkable organization. Wealth for the Common Good (wealthforcommongood.org) has studied in depth and with remarkable objectivity the issues of tax distribution. They have referenced some exemplary wealthy individuals who are leading by word and by example in advocating that the wealthy step up to the plate in addressing this critical need. Check out their site thoroughly; they too add to what I've shared with you on how wealth has already been redistributed – see "shifting responsibility."

I would be an irresponsible citizen if my only comments on deficit spending and the national debt were limited to the paragraphs above, so I must take it a bit further. We must recognize that operating our country on a perpetual deficit (adding ever more to the debt that our descendants will eventually have to pay back with crippling interest) is the epitome of self-centered shortsightedness. We DON'T have a right to do this. First we have to develop the *will* to live within our means, then we can find a *way*. We can't keep voting for politicians who promise government services at high levels and taxes at low levels. Reversing this mind-set will take a major make-over, but it is a must. If we the people get real, the politicians will have to.

I acknowledge that deficit spending right now, this year and next, is part of the economic solution. (What, other than government, is big enough to stop the downward spiral of more layoffs, less personal spending, less production, and on?) However, for Progressives to be even connected with, let alone responsible for a budget, an actual *plan*, that continues deficit spending to the tune of an average of two thirds of a trillion dollars ($660,000,000,000!) per year each year for the next eight years is irresponsible and will ultimately be political suicide. Progressives can't give such a strong hand to a far right which would use that point of irresponsibility to get back into power. Once there they could do untold damage to progress our country has made in shifting our foreign policy, taking a more responsible and farsighted approach on the environment, and going back to a mixed economy where government plays an active oversight role in avoiding economic meltdowns. The spin against the necessity of deficit spending in 2009 and '10 has already created a shift back toward conservative policies, and if we don't make the necessary tough choices to ultimately end deficit spending, that shift will continue. We can't be so foolish as to let large-scale deficit spending continue beyond the immediate economic emergency.

From 2006 through 2009 the shift has been against the excesses of the right. There are people from building contractors to custodians to store owners who had for a good while voted Republican, who came to question the party line. They have pride in their hard work, and don't like the idea of the lazy mooching off of their taxes, and that has made them conservatives. But they came to see the excesses of the elite, of the very wealthy, and they questioned their allegiance. The tide indeed shifted. However, if Progressives get carried away and continue deep deficit spending beyond 2010, and any significant deficit spending beyond 2011, the reversed tide of 2010 will only strengthen.

It doesn't have to be at one extreme or the other. Picture the numbers 1 through 10 spread in front of you, left to right. At 1 we have extremist tree huggers, those folks who have no respect for the value of jobs in the economy, and who think of any little creature as of equal value to a human life. At 10 we have corporate heavy lifters, those folks whose bottom line is "a buck now," and who have no respect for tomorrow and what it brings to all of our descendants.

It might be constructive to take a moment and reflect on which end of that spectrum 1-10 has been in power for most of the last decade, and whether or not we want it to stay that way. The extremes don't have to win if we in the middle stand up and speak up.

We need to struggle with and resolve a number of specifics along these lines. The Bush administration was right to bring our attention to the non-sustainability of the Social Security program as it now exists. The type of solution he proposed though was rejected at least in part because so many people recognized that he didn't even seriously consider other partial solutions that are reasonable. Why should Social Security deductions stop on incomes over *any* certain point? The increased SS intake if that were changed would make a substantial difference.

Some are again going to whine about that being confiscatory, but again, it simply helps look out for the stability of the broader society by having those who have *benefited* disproportionately from the free market system *support* disproportionately that same system. It doesn't argue with the fact that they can and have benefited.

 # 24. We have already made other adjustments that affect the average and poor; full SS benefits are available only at increasing ages, as it should be. If a system that was designed to look out for the broader good can make adjustments that affect the masses, surely it can make adjustments that affect the privileged.

 # 25. The need for significant adjustments to reality in programs like Medicaid and Medicare is pressing too. In the latter case it may be that we Baby Boomers need to just suck it up and realize that not everything we wish for can be.

With endless and sometimes heated discussion of doing something about our ever-escalating healthcare costs continuing, I must add here a reminder to get past beliefs and wishes. Ultimately we do have to deal with the devilish details, but far too often people tend to launch themselves into a sea of details before adequately orienting themselves to the big picture. I will touch no details here, but will attempt to help us recognize some unavoidable and fundamental realities.

Yes, we should look at every conceivable way of providing decent healthcare to everyone, and so reform *is* needed, but we can't blindly fall for the 'wouldn't it be nice' mentality; we do have to live within our means. Really! In part this may mean that we lower our expectations that doctors fix what's wrong with basically no consideration of cost. Part of this means we take more individual responsibility for our lifestyles and choices, and the natural consequences. This also means something that we never hear from politicians because they have to ask for votes; it means that we accept eventual death as part of the circle of life. I am a Baby Boomer and in little more than a decade will be an official senior citizen, but I don't believe I'm alone in recognizing that there's something distorted about the fact that not only is almost 60% of total lifetime healthcare costs spent after age 65, but "well over one-third of the average 85-year-old's expenditures lies in that person's future." (Alemayehu and Warner, *Health Services Research*, June, 2004) The distortion gets even more impressive when you look at the following graph and realize that the dollars spent to prolong life in the last few months is a description of denial.

B

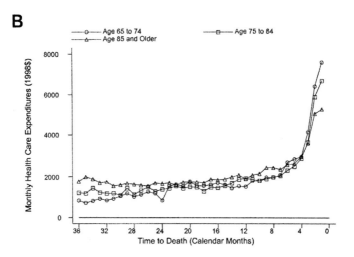

Figure 4. . (B)
Health care expenditures by time to death and age.
("Longevity and Health Care Expenditures: The Real
Reasons Older People Spend More," Yang, Norton,
and Stearns; Journal of Gerontology: SOCIAL
SCIENCES, 2003, Vol. 58B, No. 1, S2-S10)

If some wealthy people fear death so much that they'll
spend with no limit to wring a last few desperate months
out of life, well, that's how they choose to spend their
money. But if it is we, the public, who have to decide how
to spread our limited resources, are an unlimited number of
CT scans or MRIs to check up on multiple mini-strokes in
the closing months of one's life something we can actually
afford?

I'm not suggesting that doctors should capriciously
play god in trying to guess who is actually in their last six
months, but, despite the unpopularity of limited or rationed
access to healthcare, there *is* a limit to what we as a society
can actually afford, so there must be limits to procedures
that are offered on the public dollar. Does society owe

anybody this degree of expense for such short-term payoff? I am fully aware that this isn't politically correct, but we should remember that what's popular isn't always right, and what's right isn't always popular.

There are some interesting ironies in the healthcare debate. Some of the loudest voices protesting against reforming our healthcare system, currently pretty freely run by the 'market' (profit) system, are dead set against the idea of rationing or limiting services in any way. These same people are also dead set against higher taxes! This type of voter and this type of politician want unlimited Medicare access to incredibly expensive services, but they don't want to pay for it.

If we had our financial house otherwise in order, if we weren't deficit spending like there is no tomorrow, I would join those objecting to the idea of limiting health care services. Indeed, how do you place a dollar figure limit on a life? But we are a long ways from having our financial house in order! What is moral about passing on an overwhelming debt burden to our great-grandchildren just because we wanted our lives easier, and extended to the last possible moment at any price?

Another irony is that it is typically the conservative Christians among us who most loudly condemn the immorality of the idea of "letting" someone die because we can't afford to spend more on them. I would think that Christians of real faith would be pointing to their responsibility to future generations and facing near end-of-life circumstances with courage and hope and "Oh death, where is thy sting?" on their lips.

It is also interesting to examine the average senior citizen's defense of unlimited Medicare spending under one particular light. Imagine that we could set up a multigenerational accounting system; in this way the person demanding or accepting another expensive test or procedure would know they were taking money from the very account which their own grand or great-grandchildren will eventually have to pay off. Would it affect their expectations of unlimited expensive care if they actually knew they were placing a direct burden on their own descendants? I tend to think of the average grandparent as a good, non-self-centered, and at times willingly self-sacrificing person who would in no way expect his grandchildren to accept the burden of using a *credit card on the future* to pay for things that we can't really afford. Well, dear senior citizen, if you wouldn't do that to your own great-grandchildren, why would you do that to their whole generation? Please, don't put other people in the position of pointing out what we can't afford; step up to the plate yourselves and loudly and collectively demand that we reign in Medicare spending to what we can afford, to what you are comfortable asking your grandchildren to pay for.

Having mentioned that the current healthcare system is driven by the profit motive, I must add a few other big-picture observations. We don't have to resort to Communism to recognize and modify some current fundamentally mistaken principles. The raw goal of the pharmaceutical and health insurance businesses, as well as that of direct healthcare practitioners, ought to be at least somewhat different than the banking sector. There are some sectors of the economy whose sole purpose is to make money. There are (or should be) others whose primary purpose is to serve a basic human need. I'm in one such field. I teach, and most anyone would say it would be crazy to restructure education to where profit was the primary driving force. Well, isn't it ludicrous when pharmaceutical executives and upper management walk off with millions while the cost of drugs is such a big part of continually inflating healthcare's price?

It doesn't stop there. Drug reps drive cars with no limits to their private use at company expense. Where do you think they tack on those expenses? For-profit insurance companies design their every policy around what – serving the individual stricken with a health crisis, or making the most money? These realities could change with a fundamentally reformed single-payer system, but it would have to be one where we do recognize that there are limits to what we all owe to each other. If we can't accept that, we'll continue to have ridiculously underserved people at the same time as we are making other people rich almost beyond the everyday man's imagination. I predict here that the 'final' health care reform we've ended up compromising on in early 2010 won't be reform enough. We need first to adjust our expectations to the realities of what we can actually afford.

A few pages back I referred to the understandable reaction of hard-working members of our society to the excesses of the tax-and-spend left, to not liking being abused by the lazy. That's real. There are two questions though, that are sometimes not analyzed. 1. Are there any members of our society who do need and deserve our support? 2. Can you completely eliminate abuse from any large bureaucracy?

If we have the guts and callousness to answer the first with "No," then we can move on without the second. We could have an official policy of social Darwinism. If you're fit, you survive; if not, tough. If however, our answer to the first is "Yes," then we must struggle with the second.

Anyone who runs a small business with say six employees can first-handedly ensure that they are not wasteful and inefficient. But as driven and competitive as Bill Gates and most of his Microsoft employees are, he still can't ensure complete efficiency throughout a relatively large bureaucracy. This is not to say that we should sigh and accept all manner of governmental inefficiency. No! In fact we owe a debt of gratitude to the real fiscal conservatives who have battled government waste. But it is to say that the inevitable existence of some level of waste is not a good excuse for wielding a battle axe at whole programs that do address some real needs and issues of the broader good.

We who advocate for reasonable government programs to care for those who truly need the help must be on our toes though fighting to minimize abuse of such programs. Let's honestly ask ourselves if the welfare reforms begun in 1996 have gone far enough. How much abuse still happens? Check into it. Do we owe a free ride to anybody who ought to able to pull their own wagon for the most part? If we blissfully and ignorantly continue to pay out what we can't afford, particularly to those who don't need it, when we eventually get to the financial crunch which lurks around the corner if we don't change our ways, what will happen to all those legitimately needy people, to the abusers and scammers, and to you and me in that chaos?

It will be interesting to watch the far right and see if they ultimately develop a split between the extreme fiscal conservatives (who include some avowed Christians) whose politics are basically social Darwinism, and the more moderate (which includes other Christians who recognize degrees of socialism in scripture, as in Acts 4 and James for starters).

Having brought up the issues of government waste and real fiscal conservatives I can't resist raising one more challenge to middle-Americans. On many pork barrel spending attachments, voters in 49 states recognize the abuse that is going on; but voters in the one state involved go along with the ludicrous because it benefits them. It may be asking a lot, it may even border on the unrealistic, but if we all asked ourselves if the proposed project is good for more than "us," and if we were then willing to speak up in protest to our own representatives and senators, and to vote out corruption and cronyism, we might eliminate a lot of waste on our own.

A few pages back I used the terms 'capitalism' and 'free market economy', and so must comment on the lessons learned from the economic meltdown of the latter half of 2008 and early 2009. Good old-fashioned conservative ideology, expressed so simply by Ronald Reagan, says "Government's not the solution; government is the problem." But let's think deeper than clever slogans. No less a financial icon than Alan Greenspan has now confessed that his life-long assumption that markets and institutions could and would regulate themselves in their own best long-term interest has needed re-evaluation. Yes, Alan Greenspan was willing to take a hard second look at his beliefs, and to recognize that the evidence showed that "government" regulation can be part of the solution. Further, for a frightening moment imagine if the Bush administration had succeeded in privatizing Social Security; where would the crash and recession of 2008 and '09 have left that fund, and those people?

Let's also note the irony in the fact that the same group that complains most vociferously today about the bailouts for several of the big banks and insurance companies would have screamed about government interference if some years back these huge financial institutions had been denied the free market right to merge, acquire, and become so big. As we struggled with the possibility of complete meltdown, economists from the political left and right agreed that these institutions were indeed too big to (be allowed to) fail; the consequences would have been economy-shattering. Well, if we don't want to bail out some financial behemoths in the future, we must never again allow any of them to become so big that we can't let them fail. What's the only thing to keep these free market mergers and acquisitions from creating these dangerously enormous institutions? It clearly is government regulation and oversight. Some may not like it or want to accept it and change their cherished beliefs, but that doesn't change the evidence or the results of clear thinking.

Old style conservatives need a hard and honest look in the mirror. What you want to believe, what you might *wish* were so, may simply not be the case. Our county has a long if varied history of cultivating a mixed economy, one in which government regulation has a role. We will continue to argue over where to strike that balance, but we can hope we've heard the last from those advocating truly free markets with *no* regulation.

Beyond a balanced budget, a balanced approach to governance and life

In wrapping up this attempt to look toward the long-term over the immediate, toward the good of society over "me," it may be worthwhile to review at least one real case in the battle over government's role. I lived in southern California in the late 80s. We often couldn't see the San Bernardino Mountains twenty miles away; and frighteningly too often we couldn't even see the hills only two miles in the other direction. Now you can enjoy both views. The air is qualitatively and quantitatively very different. It is very unlikely that without government regulation, that change would have happened.

I now live in a relatively small town in southern Oregon. Our air used to be polluted, not by unnumbered vehicles but by unregulated wood burning. The same positive change in air quality has been accomplished here too, for the same reason. But an irony from the other side has shown its head here recently. Our county is big by almost any standard;

and our town, of still slightly fewer than 50,000 including the suburbs, is a small drop of urban life in a spacious rural landscape. Our situation was this: our landfill site was filling up, and a decision had to be made on what to do next.

Discussions of trucking our wastes over mountain passes or shipping it by rail to distant sites seemed to be all we heard or read. The inefficiency of these being obvious to me, I called to ask why, in such an area of open spaces, we couldn't just get a new and relatively local landfill site. The guy almost laughed. His reply was something like, "The number of hoops we'd have to jump through, the number of *years* it would take to get a new landfill site approved, make it basically undoable." How ironic. Laws intended to help us safeguard our environment, the same general set of laws that helped us clean up our air, are now making us do the least efficient and sensible thing with our solid waste.

The line between good government and big government isn't always obvious and is easily crossed. The left tends to want tons of government; the right tends to want no government except an army. To these two extreme segments who have unthinking loyalty to a party line and know what they believe, add a here-to-fore too silent middle, and a media which likes to create neat categories (red vs. blue and such) where reality shows complexities involving single-digit differences, and you have a recipe for governance from the extremes. It is time that **We** changed that.

26. It is up to all of us to make sure that government is and does the right thing.

POSTSCRIPT

Among the various criticisms that may well be aimed at things I've said, one might be that I've simply jumped on the bandwagon that from 2005 through 2009 was going against conservative policies, particularly as most recently manifested by the Bush administration. To nip that notion in the bud, I am including here a copy of a guest editorial I wrote before the election of 2004, when conservatives still held sway. It was my first step in ending my silence. I've continued to write and speak out ever since, and this book is simply the culmination of those efforts to get us really thinking, not just blindly believing and following.

After this editorial I will share some final remarks on the current political pendulum swing vs. really learning the deeper lessons.

The following was published as an Op-Ed in the *Herald and News* of Klamath Falls, Oregon, on October 4, 2004.

U.S. still has a chance with Arabs, Muslims who are open-minded
But President Bush's policies have been a failure.
By Doug Matheson

President Bush has rhetorically asked if the world is safer, if we feel safer, as a result of his removing Saddam Hussein from power. In uncertain and threatening times many of us are giving him the credit he claims for making us safer. My life experience in various countries, particularly in the Middle East, leads me to conclude otherwise, and I write this article to point out several ways in which he continues to make our world a significantly less safe place.

When we went into Afghanistan to take out al-Qaida following 9-11, the world at large not only understood, they were with us. But as this administration plowed stubbornly ahead with plans to invade Iraq, we left much of the world behind. More significantly, large portions of the non-extremist Arab/Muslim world, which did have decades of reasons for frustration with - but not hatred for - us, shifted ominously away from us. When we could have shown determination, perseverance, patience and persistence in slowly gathering international resolve to make Saddam cooperate or be removed, we took the short cut. The Bush administration knew what it <u>wanted</u> the intelligence to show, and got their way. If President Bush had even listened to some of the more even-handed (Colin Powell instead of Dick Cheney) within his own circle he would have persisted longer in gathering a broader coalition who saw the need for strong action. Instead we acted, in the eyes of much of the world, alone. So what have we gained, and what have we lost?

We did depose a genuinely bad guy; but in ignorance of and condescending treatment toward a proud people from an ancient civilization, this administration stuck with its preferred simple "black and white" viewpoint and didn't begin to anticipate how truly complex and difficult establishing peace would be. We lost the position that America goes to war only when absolutely necessary. We gained legions of people who used to mistrust us who now hate us... and tragically could for generations. Safer world? I wish he were right, but am sure that in the long run it's the opposite.

One thing I expect of our country's leadership is the ability to see the long view, not just the immediate, to see beyond its own cultural heritage, not just "the world according to me." Was bad-guy Saddam an imminent threat worth sacrificing America's reputation for fairness? (Though that reputation was questionable in some places and ways, we still had the benefit of the doubt in most of the world.) The answer is no, though unfortunately it may take living through the threats and acts of legions of committed terrorists (a growing al-Qaida as opposed to a dwindling one) for us to see that the answer was no.

Our leadership needs to be wise enough to take it to terrorists without adding unnecessary fuel to the fire. It is extremist Muslims, not normal Muslims, who form the core of al-Qaida. Our leadership should be minimizing the degree to which extremists can use religious differences to inflame, motivate, and recruit. Yet George Bush, showing the same primitive and arrogant attitude as Osama bin Laden, says things like "I don't need the approval of my father, I seek the approval of a higher authority" and "I believe I am President because it is God's will" and "I believe it is God's will that I be President again." Those kinds of statements, that kind of attitude, are simply unnecessary fuel to the terrorist's fire. Why go there? Keep in mind that in less educated societies, the people at large naturally label enemy groups (us) with the attributes they see in our leaders. The leadership flavors their whole perception.

I would respect a leader simply saying "I sincerely seek to do right, I do seek God's guidance," but actually claiming to be president because it is God's will is amazing. Although I wasn't able to stomach voting for Al Gore in the last election, what does Mr. Bush imply about everyone who didn't vote for him? Are they the devil's agents, or simply out of tune with God and His will?

While I found it initially incomprehensible why our President is so public with his religion, I have come to see two possibilities. One, he may simply have so little experience in the broader world that he may be ignorant of the potential for unnecessarily inflaming things. Two, he knows most of us (2 of 3 we're told) initially reflexively respond positively to a politician's expressions of faith. Maybe he simply figures the added risk of inflaming and motivating more terrorists is worth the gathered votes.

The Founding Fathers of our nation had the wisdom to separate church and state. History is full of conflicts that have killed millions, all in the name of God. We must learn; we can't keep stumbling down that road. We elect a CEO to a democracy which welcomes faiths of all kinds, or none at all. I know we are a largely Christian nation, and that most of you reading this are Christians of one type or another and many believe in sharing your faith, but being president puts you under different obligations. No one would mind our President going to church, Bible study, or prayer meeting, but he should keep it to himself and his fellow worshipers. His personal faith and belief ought to be just that… personal. And he ought to have the wisdom to not inflame a conflict that puts our kids at increased risk to growing ranks of terrorists by bringing his religious experience to the forefront. Being the head of state in an open society, wisely designed to keep church and state separate, means one's personal faith is personal.

In the years I have lived in other countries, I've found people to be very gracious in separating American policies from American individuals. Unfortunately, terrorists have forgotten that. In our fight with terrorists we are going to have to be tough and perseverant, but even more we are also going to have to be wise in finding ways to narrow their base and not broaden their appeal. I hope with all my heart that we can show to the many still potentially open-minded Arabs/Muslims that we, the American people, millions of American individuals, are different from recent American policy. Let's vote Mr. Bush out.

* * *

Before wrapping this book up, I feel the need to explain ever having written something like "Although I wasn't able to stomach voting for Al Gore in the last election…" I did what I now consider to be a gutless thing in the 2000 election; I cast a vote on all other issues and people on my ballot, but I simply didn't vote for anybody for president because I had strong reservations on George Bush and I felt then that Al Gore was a bit too extreme on environmental issues. An honest confession on this issue is that I teach in an area that then supported Mr. Bush by about 85%, and I felt that actually voting for Al Gore would make people in my sphere of influence tune my voice completely out. I now believe that the courageous and right thing to have done in that election would have meant voting for Al Gore, but that's hindsight.

Now to put a final wrap on this book – let's look briefly at the elections of 2008 and 2010. With prominent Republicans in various corners admitting out loud that Bush had dug his party into a pretty deep hole, it was a safe bet that the 2006 shifts to Democratic majorities in Congress would only strengthen. It was also likely, though some argued it was a less certain bet, that then Senator Obama would also take the White House for the Democrats. Now that the election is history, those bets look like we should have seen a sure thing. But why?

Unfortunately, the answers are as shallow as is typical for political pendulum swings. First, the economy in mid

2008 looked shaky, and then nearly tanked as the election neared. Historically, presidents and their party get too much credit and too much blame for the fluctuations which a free market economy inevitably has. Second, we were truly tired of the war in Iraq; and, with or without clear analysis of what was wrong with the various decisions, we were going against the group most closely connected with putting us there.

In 2010 voters were apparently most frustrated with continued high unemployment and the relatively slow pace of the broad economic recovery. Remember the disproportionate credit and/or blame which presidents and their party get? Add to that the whirlwind of spin around whether or not health care reform was a good thing, or went too far, or not far enough. The last few elections were primed for reactionary votes, and didn't disappoint. It may take several years or even decades, but someday we may come to review and eventually reverse the Supreme Court's *Citizens United v. Federal Election Commission* decision that unlimited corporate money somehow equals free speech. Behind the spin on many issues and races are puppet strings made of dollar bills, and the puppeteers want reactionary votes, not thoughtful ones.

Shouldn't we put honest effort into doing more than reacting, into thinking deeper? There are, after all, lessons of lasting import to be learned. Pendulum swings between liberal and conservative in many areas are interesting and may even make for some heated arguments, but in the big picture are relatively inconsequential. We're not going to opt for a Communist state, and we're not going to allow robber baron monopolists free reign, so the debate on taxes and spending and on government's role will go on. Even something as sensitive as abortion isn't going to shape the future, and so again the debate goes on.

But on several fronts the dangers of a recently influential and still-plotting group can have enormously grave consequences. One of these fronts is our approach to the world. We could call it foreign policy. The recently influential group is the neoconservatives. If you question this I would suggest again that you read the "Project for the New American Century." While reading, be sure to try putting yourself in the shoes of a citizen of any other country. Certain ideas sound innocent enough to begin with, even appealing. Take for example "… increase defense spending," and "provide a secure basis for U.S. power projection around the world." But then it goes further: "ensure the long-term superiority of U.S. conventional forces." Even this can sound innocuous if you look at it through narrowly American eyes.

However, if you really imagine the perspective of anybody else, the deliberate plan to be singularly the most powerful, and to project that power to being "superior," is understandably scary. It ought to be a "duh" moment to realize that the neo-con approach to the world is a sure-fire formula for steadily losing friends and turning previously neutral parties into committed enemies. (My last recommendation on insightful reading comes in this area of constructive vs. destructive engagement in our world. Samantha Power's *A Problem from Hell: America and the Age of Genocide* will inform and challenge you.)

A second front with potential for grave consequences is the environment. This is clearly a paraphrase, but the same far conservative approach seems to have been "Don't get in the way of business with regulations, let people make a buck now. If your imaginary problems do become a reality, we'll deal with that then." They fail to recognize that the "we" who will have to deal with the degraded environment will be their own grandchildren, and the rest of humanity.

In seeking to leave our great-grandchildren a stable planet, sociologically, ecologically, and economically, we must never again fall for some far conservative positions. President Bush chose to embrace severely damaging conservative positions on foreign policy, on the environment, and on a third front – the role of government in overseeing business. Those are deep reasons to shift allegiances, but this must not be just another temporary pendulum swing.

Although the elections of 2000, 2004, 2006, 2008, and 2010 have been mentioned in this book, the purpose for my writing goes far beyond recent or near-future elections. We don't need a swing of the pendulum. As the election of Scott Brown to the vacant Massachusetts Senate seat in early 2010 showed, the winds behind the various swings of the pendulum can shift in a heartbeat. And as the fall 2010 election shows, some winds can blow with surprising intensity, at least for the moment. I personally applaud the Tea Party folk for their emphasis on cutting government spending and living within our means. I find it ridiculous though that so many of these same people forget their own broad generalization when it comes to specifics; they want to keep their Social Security, their Medicare, and their infinite military. Further, I find any suggestions that we should cut our taxes before we pay off the national debt absolutely self-serving. Future generations don't owe us such a luxury. It will likely take a couple of decades, and our national debt (not deficit) should be expressed in billions not trillions, before we can responsibly talk about cutting our taxes. Yes, we need to operate with a surplus for a good number of years, steadily paying down our debt, and not complain about it! But that means leaving our taxes up there while bringing our spending down to match, and then taking it lower still. I use the words "leaving our taxes up there" advisedly because *relative* to the rest of the world and to the moral demand to not bury our descendants in debt, our taxes are **not** 'up there' to an inordinate degree. Our spending though certainly has been, and that must change.

Instead of another pendulum swing, what we need is a shift away from loyal *belief* toward real *thinking* (honestly processing information), and a change in our posture and attitude toward each other. We need to take ownership of the consequences that our leaders' actions bring – we put those leaders in power. We must get better at seeing through distortion and spin in the media, and we must not get locked in to one position forever. If we learn to do more than just hold our beliefs, if we learn to stay open to new information, to really question and analyze, and to adjust our thinking and conclusions when necessary, we'll be so much more likely to create a great future for our great-grandchildren and their peers.

Behind the recent neo-con errors on the fronts of foreign policy, the environment, and the role of government is the common ground of cocky, self-centered, me-now, I-know-it-all, our-country-is-best-and-deserves-most, absolutist attitude and set of firmly fixed beliefs. If we the people monitor ourselves and avoid that tempting infection, we will choose leaders with a different posture who will put different (evidence based and thought through) policy in place. We can and must shift without ever swinging back to shallow and temporary positions on these big-picture items.

Appendix A

I hold these truths to be self-evident:

That each culture has its own traditions about the earth, man, the universe, and its God(s).

That no faith is any more objectively verifiable than any other.

That we should hold our faiths with humility, and respect others' faiths.

That faith is a personal matter in which the state has no business.

That we will have some enemies we did nothing to earn.

That we can inadvertently make other enemies by our words, attitude, approach, posture, and our actions.

That we must defend ourselves when our enemies are of the first variety, and learn when of the second variety.

That the forward march of civilization has been driven by and gained from an application of the scientific method; that we figure things out, improve our ideas and our technology, through gathering and analyzing evidence, and adjusting our conclusions.

That our ideas, our understanding of things, should match up with verifiable evidence.

That if there is conflict between what we believe and what the evidence says, we should be willing to change our conclusions, to let our previous beliefs lose and the evidence win.

That we all share one atmosphere, one ocean, and one planet.

That what is good for our country in the long run, necessarily takes into consideration what is good for humanity as a whole.

That equality of opportunity is a goal worth striving for generation after generation.

That if we think and act only for the immediate and only for ourselves, the world at large is likely to become a decidedly less stable place.

That the free enterprise system works much better than communism, and that those who benefit disproportionately from this system should also support this system disproportionately.

That we owe a decent, stable, and enjoyable world to future generations.

That in all our personal and collective choices, we should think beyond "me, now."

Appendix B

	Share of Capital Income Flowing to Households in Various Income Categories							
	Bottom 20 percent	Second 20 percent	Middle 20 percent	Fourth 20 percent	Top 20 percent	Top 10 percent	Top 5 percent	Top 1 percent
1979	1.8%	4.1%	6.7%	10.5%	76.5%	66.7%	57.9%	37.8%
1980	1.8%	3.9%	7.0%	11.3%	75.5%	65.0%	55.6%	35.6%
1981	1.6%	3.8%	7.1%	11.9%	74.9%	64.6%	55.4%	35.8%
1982	1.7%	4.0%	7.5%	12.1%	73.8%	63.3%	54.9%	37.7%
1983	1.6%	3.8%	7.5%	12.2%	74.2%	63.7%	55.2%	37.6%
1984	1.9%	3.8%	7.5%	12.7%	73.2%	63.5%	55.1%	38.5%
1985	1.4%	3.7%	7.5%	12.3%	74.2%	64.9%	56.9%	39.7%
1986	1.4%	3.3%	7.2%	11.7%	75.7%	67.4%	59.5%	42.8%
1987	1.3%	3.8%	7.7%	12.8%	73.1%	64.0%	55.3%	36.7%
1988	1.2%	3.4%	7.5%	11.6%	74.9%	66.5%	58.4%	40.7%
1989	1.2%	3.6%	7.0%	11.7%	75.2%	66.0%	57.4%	39.1%
1990	1.2%	3.2%	6.9%	11.6%	75.6%	66.3%	57.4%	39.7%
1991	1.4%	3.4%	7.5%	11.6%	74.5%	64.7%	56.2%	38.3%
1992	1.3%	3.2%	6.9%	10.8%	76.4%	67.8%	59.0%	40.7%
1993	1.1%	3.0%	6.3%	10.3%	77.9%	69.2%	60.5%	42.2%
1994	1.0%	2.7%	6.2%	10.1%	78.5%	70.0%	62.1%	44.5%
1995	1.1%	2.6%	5.9%	10.0%	79.0%	70.1%	61.5%	43.2%
1996	0.9%	2.4%	5.8%	9.7%	80.1%	71.2%	62.4%	44.5%
1997	0.8%	2.2%	5.3%	9.2%	81.5%	72.6%	64.1%	45.7%
1998	0.8%	2.2%	5.4%	8.7%	82.0%	73.8%	65.4%	47.9%
1999	0.8%	2.2%	5.5%	8.5%	82.1%	73.8%	65.7%	47.8%
2000	0.9%	2.1%	5.3%	8.0%	82.9%	74.6%	66.5%	49.1%
2001	0.7%	2.0%	4.8%	8.5%	82.6%	74.8%	67.8%	51.8%
2002	0.6%	1.8%	4.3%	8.0%	83.4%	76.0%	69.5%	53.4%
2003	0.6%	1.5%	3.7%	6.9%	85.9%	79.5%	73.3%	57.6%
2004	0.6%	1.5%	3.0%	6.5%	87.3%	81.4%	74.7%	59.5%
2005	0.6%	1.4%	3.0%	6.2%	87.8%	81.6%	74.9%	58.6%

from CBO Historical Effective Tax Rates: http://www.cbo.gov/doc.cfm?index=8885
This table is based on the second part (entitled "Share of Corporate Tax Liabilities")
of Table 2, Shares of Federal Tax Liabilities for All Households, by Comprehensive
Household Income Category, 1979 to 2005
Historical Effective Tax Rates, 1979 to 2005: Supplement with Additional Data on
Sources of Income and High-Income Households December 23, 2008 pdf data)

About the Author

Watching the fabric of civilization begin to unravel and the genocide unfold in Rwanda in 1994, Doug Matheson witnessed major societal convulsions. He saw a lesser example of the same in Beirut, Lebanon, in 1980-81. Being present during this type of chaos could be considered a misfortune, but, from a learning perspective, he has turned it into an opportunity.

The process of really learning from life requires at least: careful observation, honest questioning and weighing of evidence, and a willingness to change your mind when warranted. In short, this means being willing to move beyond what you happen to believe. Matheson grew up the child of missionaries with a clearly defined set of beliefs. Learning to question, to analyze, to re-evaluate, to *think*, to change, to grow, has been a life-long process for him.

Applying the learned habits from his career as a science educator to honestly evaluating humanity's current circumstances and challenges has led him to cease being a silent citizen. He points out that our times are a strange mix of privilege and peril. In filling what he sees as all of our roles as responsible adults to "leave a decent, stable, and enjoyable world to future generations," he draws on an unusually diverse life experience.

Besides Lebanon and Rwanda, he has also lived in Canada, India, Singapore, and France. Applying thinking, not just believing, to this breadth of life experience has given him insight into how America is perceived around the world, the mix of distortion and reality behind those perceptions, the results of our actions in the world, and much about the broader human circumstance.

As a no-longer-silent citizen of the United States, he brings the same objective thinking to a number of critical internal political matters. He's honest, and therefore not always politically correct.

To respond, participate in dialog, or
buy a book for a friend, visit
actuallythinking.com

CPSIA information can be obtained at www.ICGtesting.com
Printed in the USA
BVOW040228010512

289044BV00001B/1/P